Carving
and
Boning
Like an
Expert

Oreste Carnevali

with Jean B. Read

Illustrations by Pat Stewart

Carving
and
Boning
Like an
Expert

Random House   New York

Library of Congress Cataloging in Publication Data
Carnevali, Oreste.
Carving and boning like an expert.
1. Carving (Meat, etc.)   2. Meat—Boning.
I. Read, Jean B., joint author. II. Title.
TX885.C37   642'.6   77-90298
ISBN 0-394-41960-X
ISBN 0-394-73412-2 pbk.

Manufactured in the United States of America
Design by Bernard Klein
24689753
First Edition

Contents

Carving Lamb

Carving Pork

Carving Veal

Boning Fish and Lobster

Carving Vegetables

Carving Fruit

Introduction by James Beard

I can remember the days when a knowledge of carving was considered to be part of the training of an accomplished gentleman. Traditionally, carving was regarded as an integral part of a good education, and in noble households a master of carving was the last tutor provided for the sons of the family.

In Edwardian times, one of the features of a great dinner party was watching the host perform with a knife on a bird or joint, expertly separating flesh from bone and serving perfect slices to his guests. This skill was handed down from father to son, and there was no end of fuss about having the proper knives and sharpening steels laid out, the right platter or board on which to carve, and someone standing attentively by to receive the plates of carved meat and distribute them to the guests.

Alas, this came to an end, along with other rituals of the table, and carelessness was the keynote of carving in most households. Men no longer considered it their prerogative and their pride. While there were a number of women who had a deft way with a knife and took over the job in the kitchen, performing, on the whole, remarkably well, they never pulled it off with quite the flourish of the old paterfamilias.

The art of *découpage,* as carving is known in France, requires not only a knowledge of the anatomy of bird or beast but also constant practice to bring it to perfection. Within the last few years I have been delighted to notice a resurgence of interest in good carving, which seems to go hand in hand with the rise in popularity of couples cooking together. The pleasure men are now finding in the kitchen seems to have furthered their interest in carving, and the standards are quite a lot higher than they used to be. I am probably more conscious of this because within the last two years I have punctuated my regular cooking classes with carving classes, at which I asked Oreste Carnevali to demonstrate his prowess to a group of interested students, for in my opinion, this is one art of the table where it is impossible to attain perfection without having the opportunity to observe and work with a master carver. Never have I announced a class that was subscribed to so quickly. It seemed everyone wanted to be in on the act, and I could have filled the classes several times over.

I have known and worked with Oreste over a long span of years and have marveled at the skill and utter relaxation with which he tackles anything from a tiny quail to a large turkey or a saddle of venison. Never have I seen him falter for a second. He has a thorough knowledge of bone structure, an unerring eye and his own graceful style of turning a bird or roast into a beautiful platter of perfectly disjointed or sliced meat. At a recent Thanksgiving dinner at the Four Seasons in New York, the restaurant which is Oreste's home grounds, there were two small turkeys to be carved at our table. I took my attention from my guests and watched Oreste's performance with total fascination. It was smooth, efficient, and while by no means showy or flamboyant, could only be termed theatrical in terms of grace and consummate artistry. I have known Oreste to break with classic rules, but in so doing he establishes his own rules, for he is one of the great carvers of our time.

In this book Oreste is not attempting to be a showman. He approaches his subject from the point of view of the person who is faced with the necessity of carving a bird or a piece of meat efficiently, attractively, and with a minimum of effort, dealing not only with the familiar birds and cuts of meat, but also with the game birds and animals that present a more difficult problem for the average person. He also covers boning and presenting fish, and elegantly deals with fruit and vegetables at table. He wastes no motion, he wields his fork and knife with the confidence and deftness of a master, and if you follow what he does faithfully, you too can acquire confidence and skill. To carve and arrange meat on a plate or platter so that it is mouth-watering and appealing to the eye is as necessary a part of being a good cook as the proper preparation of food. I feel that this is a universal handbook for anyone who is truly interested in the arts of the table.

Preface

Restaurants have been a part of my life ever since I can remember. In Mantua, the town in northern Italy where I was born, for three generations the Carnevali family have run what Italians call a *locanda*, or what Americans would recognize as a country inn.

As little children, my brother and I used to play in the restaurant kitchen, stopping to watch our mother chop up bits of ham for a risotto—if she was not too rushed, we might get a bite. But if we were slow to stand back when she opened the big oven door to baste a roast of veal or tap the crusty surface of a batch of bread, pronto—out we would go.

By the age of eleven I began to take an interest in food beyond how to spell the names of the northern Italian dishes my brother and I had to write out on the daily menus. I wanted to know how to prepare them. As time went on, we children all helped out in the kitchen. Even my little sister did small jobs, measuring out the pasta or helping to scrub vegetables, kneeling on a stool at the marble sink. By the time I was sixteen I was doing the shopping for the restaurant. Early in the morning I would go out to inspect the line of beef, lamb and fresh-killed chickens hanging in the big open-air market. Soon I too was pinching and poking the meat like the most knowledgeable and skeptical of customers. You could say that I was already well on my way to joining the family business. And I might be there yet if it had not been for an itchy foot and a big desire to see the world.

The foundation of what I know comes from those early years, especially a sound respect for the art of preparing and serving food. Some fifteen years ago, I was on my honeymoon in Montreal. I was out of work and hoped to get to the States, which the Voice of America had told me was the land of opportunity. One day, I saw a Help Wanted ad for a dining room captain at the Montreal Ritz. Happy that such a good job was available in such a fine hotel, I kissed my beautiful Swedish bride and rushed off to be interviewed. All went well in the beginning. The pay was good and the maître d' in charge of the staff seemed like a decent fellow. But as he began to show me around I learned that the practice there was to bring everything in from the kitchen on a serving plate. I took a deep breath and refused the job. It was too hard to reconcile such indifference with the loving ritual of carving and serving I had learned at home.

Some of what I know also comes from the hotel school in Stresa that I went to after I left home. But I picked up far more in the hotels and restaurants where I later worked by following closely in the footsteps of the experts and watching what they did.

The restaurant I liked the best was the Pocardi in Paris. It was run by Italians and became my home away from home in a strange city. To speak my own language again and to serve dishes familiar since childhood—what a comfort! At the Pocardi, I learned to do tableside cooking, the most dramatic, satisfying and hazardous of ways to prepare food. As a beginner, my pulse would leap to the double as the flame from the spirit lamp rose and the pasta began to bubble in the chafing dish. Would I be able to get it to the serving plate? Or would a strand of linguine settle slowly in the wine glass of the gentleman who was obviously going to pay the bill—and give the tip?

I became an expert carver largely through experience, although I had a certain advantage from the start: I was already on familiar terms with many of the meats and poultry that we maître d's carve. Pigs, chickens and an occasional goose or duckling were raised behind our house, and we children knew very well what went on before a succulent loin of pork or a stuffed goose reached the family table. The shape of a butchered pig or a plucked chicken was as much a part of our lives as the landscape beyond the kitchen window.

The fact is that not many Americans are this closely acquainted with what they carve. Ever since I came to this country it has surprised me how few people know how to go about it. Although the host will make a great business of sharpening the edge of his knife, he often chooses the wrong one, and seldom follows through with the proper technique in using it. I have seen him use a sharp slicing knife to cut into an exquisite striped bass, destroying the beautiful grain, or press a two-tined carving fork (which should be banished from every American home) deep into a roast of beef, squandering the juices before the first guest is served.

What also surprises me is that in the United States carving appears to be the prerogative of the male, one that is as jealously guarded as if it were the very seal of his manhood. In our home, Mamma, like most European women, did the carving. Only on special occasions when a goose or a whole baby lamb was served did my father preside at the carving board. The truth is, I suppose, that he had more than his share of jobs like this in the restaurant.

Whoever does the carving in your home, I would like to show you, men and women alike, single and married, how to carve and bone the meats, poultry and fish that appear on your table. Given a knife and fork, anyone can hack away at a roast and come up with the necessary number of servings. Expert carving is another matter. It is not a technique that you can acquire all at once. Like developing a good backhand at tennis, or a flexible bowing arm on the violin, it takes practice. The important thing is to learn the proper procedures. Ease and skill in handling your tools will come as you grow accustomed to them, and after a while you will become an expert.

Before the sixteenth century, very little thought was given to carving. When the Romans dined, they ate with their fingers, using a crude knife to slash a choice piece from the carcass. It was not until the Medicis, when cutlery and tableware were perfected, that carving came into its own. Since then certain traditional ways of dividing up the various cuts and kinds of meat have developed. They may differ slightly from country to country, but they all have their basis in the structure of the cut, in getting the most from whatever it is you are carving, and in producing servings which are as attractive and appetizing as possible. For instance, it makes no real difference whether you remove the tenderloin whole from a saddle of lamb and then slice it, or whether you do the slicing while the tenderloin is still ·attached to the roast. It is all a matter of local tradition and personal preference. In this book I have described alternative ways of carving wherever they seem useful.

In looking at the illustrations in this book, remember that the position of the viewer and the carver are reversed. For instance, if the carver in the illustration is removing a tenderloin from the left side of a center bone, it will appear to you, the viewer, as the right side of the bone. So, to avoid mistakes, every time you look at an illustration put yourself mentally in the position of the carver.

Equipment
and General Information

Knives

Next to experience, a set of quality stainless steel knives is the most important thing in becoming a skilled carver. Such a set will cost you quite a lot of money, but you will find that the investment pays off over the years. A less expensive knife, one made of carbon steel, may appear to work well at first, but it will lose its edge quickly, and it tends to stain and rust easily. The surface of the blade will also corrode unless you give it a good deal of care.

Why is a stainless steel knife so expensive? The answer is that the process of making it is long and complicated. To make the blade alone requires five successive steps: the forging from bars of red-hot steel; the hardening and tempering by bringing the rough blade to a temperature as high as 1740°F.; the cooling, reheating and cooling again to reduce the hardness and give the blade just the right degree of flexibility and toughness; then the grinding and polishing of the blade under water to keep its temper, followed by successively finer operations of hand-glazing and buffing to give the blade its finish.

There are two ways of grinding a knife blade. One is the hollow-ground, the other the taper-ground. The hollow-ground blade is thinned at a point just behind the final edge in an attempt to reduce "drag." However, this process also tends to create a weak spot in the blade, and for this reason I don't recommend the hollow-ground knife. In taper grinding the knife is thinned consistently from the top of the blade to the edge and from the heel of the knife to the point, giving a uniform and smooth taper.

The final operation in the making of a knife is the careful attachment of the handle, which determines the balance of the knife—what the craftsman calls "the mating of the blade." With the exception of the shorter paring knife, any good knife has three rivets attaching the handle to the blade, assuring a permanent marriage between the two.

What determines the knife's staying power is the quality of the steel used in its production and the skill with which the steel is handled during the manufacturing. So, the next time you see the high price tag on a fine knife, you will understand why.

Illustrated below are the knives that I use in my kitchen. The 4″ paring knife **(A)** is used for peeling the fruits and vegetables that garnish the meats from the carving board. The 4–6″ boning knife **(B),** with its pointed tip for making incisions, is used for boning chicken, duck or squab. Of course, you can use it for boning larger cuts of meat, if you want to do that job yourself. Next to this is a light 8″ chopping knife **(C),** followed by a heavier 8″ knife **(D),** also used for chopping. After these is a chef's or butcher's knife with a blade 10″ long and about 2″ wide **(E),** and a fairly firm slicing knife with a pointed blade 11″ long **(F).** Then come a smoked salmon knife with a flexible 12″ blade, blunt-tipped **(G),** a general-purpose serrated slicing knife with a 12″ blade **(H),** and a cleaver for chopping **(I).** Finally, there is an apple corer and the larger pineapple corer **(J).**

It is not absolutely necessary that you acquire all these knives at once. After all, for centuries the Chinese have produced an extraordinary cuisine with only one knife—the cleaver. But if I could have only four of the above to equip my carving board I would choose the paring knife, the light 8″ chopping knife, the 11″ slicing knife for thin slicing of foods like flank steak or smoked salmon, and the serrated slicing knife for slicing anything from a turkey breast to tomatoes for garnish. You could say that these are the basic cutlery for the beginning carver.

For boning fish you will need a palette fish knife and a fish fork, which are illustrated below. As you can see, the fish knife is shaped more like a spade than a knife, and lacks a keen-edged blade. This is because the motions used in boning fish are

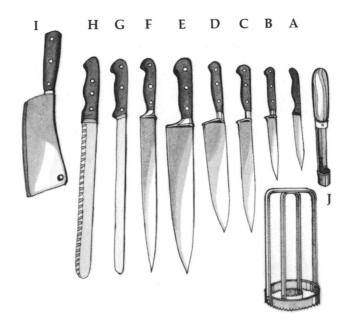

very different from the ones used in cutting meat. Instead of cutting and sawing, you will be using the palette knife to nudge and coax the flesh from the bones. The width of the fish fork helps to support the filet as you remove it.

Sharpening and Care: No matter how much you pay for your knives they are not going to last without the proper sharpening technique and careful storage. So, if you were given an electric knife sharpener last Christmas by some well-meaning relative or friend, put it away in your highest cupboard and forget about it. The same goes for the most abysmal of all gadgets, the electric carving knife. The less said about it the better. It does not even deserve mention under the heading of Knives. You can also throw out the two-wheeled sharpening device with a handle, or the slot sharpener you bought at the five-and-dime store. They will only ruin your knives. The safest and most effective method for sharpening a knife, that is, realigning its edge, is with a whetstone, the block of carborundum that is available in most stores that sell kitchen equipment. The one I use is $3\frac{1}{2}''\times 8''\times 1''$, large enough to accommodate most knives. The stone comes in varying textures. For general use, I recommend the finest grain.

To use the stone, place a drop of mineral oil on it, then pick up the knife to be sharpened in your right hand. Rest the two middle fingers on your left hand on the end of the blade and draw it back at a slight angle the length of the stone (1). Repeat this motion several times. Now turn the blade over, and starting at the bottom corner of the stone, push it slowly and firmly up to the top of the stone. Check your edge and repeat if necessary. Keep the stone covered with a cloth in a drawer.

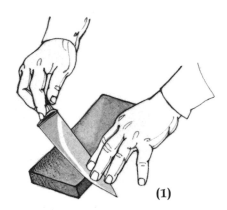

(1)

An alternative method of sharpening your knives is with the metal sharpener with a handle (called a "steel") that generally comes with a carving set. If you are going out to buy one, try to get one that has a flat surface on either side, rather than the old-fashioned kind shaped like a rod. The flat surface is preferable because it covers more of the blade.

To use the steel, take it in your left hand and the knife in your right (2).

(2)

Stroke the knife away from your body the length of the steel on one side, covering the length of the blade **(3)**. Repeat on the other side of the steel to cover the other side of the blade. Four to five strokes on each side are usually enough to get a sharp edge. It is a good idea to use the steel each time you use a knife, or at least weekly, to keep the edge of the blade in good alignment.

(3)

Not all professional carvers will agree with my recommendations on how to sharpen knives. But the ways described above are the ones that have worked best for me over the years. Some experts may also wonder why I have not gone into the technique of putting a new edge on a knife. This is because I believe the job is better and more safely done by a professional.

There are two reasons why it matters where and how you store your knives: to protect the blade itself, and to keep people from getting cut. For this reason, I am against knife racks no matter how high they are placed. Knives are attractive to children, and little ones like to climb. The magnetic rack is even more hazardous than the slotted kind. One jolt to the handle and the knife will fall. By far the best and safest place to store your knives is in a special drawer with slots. If you haven't such a storage place, use the plastic covers in which the knives came from the store, and keep them in a drawer apart from other utensils.

Another point to remember in prolonging the life of your knives: never use them for any purpose other than the one they were so painstakingly made for. Don't, for instance, use them for cutting off the tops of packaged foods, prizing lids or removing the foil from the top of a wine bottle. This kind of misuse will very quickly ruin a well-tempered blade.

Wash your knives, whether they are made of stainless or ordinary steel, by hand in hot water and soap as soon as possible after using them. If you find it more convenient to use a detergent, be sure that it is entirely dissolved in hot dishwater before you put in the knife. However, since some detergents contain an ingredient that in the presence of salt will cause instantaneous corrosion, it is best to stick with a plain soap. Prolonged soaking even in soapless water will also cause corrosion. And whatever you do, *don't put your knives in the dishwasher,* where they can become nicked and dulled, or cut the unlucky person who is unloading the washer.

If you are using a steel knife that is not stainless, clean it when necessary with a dry steel-wool pad to remove the stains, and be sure to dry it thoroughly after each use.

The Carving Board

My own carving boards are made of maple, and that is the kind I recommend that you buy. Because it is a hard wood, maple has a longer life than a wood such as teak. It is durable enough so the board can also be used for chopping; it won't slide, and properly cared for, it should last you a long time.

When you buy your board be sure to get one with a trench to catch the juices. It will help to keep your tablecloth clean, and it also gives you a nice little reservoir from which to spoon the juices over the carved meat to keep it moist.

The shape of the board is immaterial—oval or rectangular, whichever strikes your fancy. The latter type gives you a little more room because of the corners. Since you are going to have more than one board, perhaps you will want to choose one of each.

One sure way of shortening the life of any carving board, maple or teak, rectangular or oval, is to immerse it in water. The wood will swell, and you will never again have an even surface to work on. Or, if the board is laminated, you will soon find yourself with nothing but a little pile of kindling wood. If your board gets wet, and this can happen to the best of us, wipe it dry immediately. After each use, brush off the bits of meat and wipe away the juices with damp paper towels. Every few weeks go over it with more towels dipped in vegetable oil to preserve the wood. Store the board in a place where dust will not accumulate on the oiled surface.

One thing you should know about a carving board is never to put it directly on a glass or marble or highly polished wood table. It will not only scratch the surface, but there is a real danger of losing your roast. Not long ago, this happened to me, not at work but at home on a new dining room table. Fortunately, my audience was young and not too critical, but my wife was not happy about the scratches. Now I slip a dampened napkin under the board before I begin to carve.

How many boards you will want depends on your budget, the variety of carving you do, and your addiction to the beauty of wood. As you begin to perfect your technique in carving, it's very likely that your interest in carving boards will progress at the same rate. We should warn you that they *can* become an addiction. The grain of the wood, its age and origin, whether or not a board is hand-crafted: any of these factors provide an excuse to add just one more to one's collection. However, in the beginning a board big enough to accommodate a turkey or a good-sized standing roast, about 16"x18", and a smaller one, about 10"x14", should do.

Serving

How a roast chicken or a leg of lamb is served is almost as important as how it is carved. So, along with the work of carving or boning, we have illustrated or told you how to arrange each cut on the serving platter or plate.

In transferring a piece of meat from the platter, don't spear it with the fork and let it dangle in the air to land sprawling on the serving plate. Lift it gently between fork and serving spoon or carving knife, and lay it out carefully on the plate. Whatever you are serving, give your motions a low profile.

Think of the serving as the finale to your production at the carving board. A few carefully arranged slices of meat, set off with an artfully placed sprig of parsley or watercress and a vegetable in season, can be a joy to behold. In serving meat, the plate should always be presented so that the slices are close to the eater, with the vegetables on the other side of the plate. Remember that fish is always presented with the backbone toward the guests. An overloaded plate is neither artistic nor elegant and only dulls the appetite. A plate or a platter whose edges are spotted with bits of meat or gravy is likely to take it away altogether. So pay attention while you are serving, and keep the plates clean and tidy. Have a damp napkin on hand to wipe away any spills along the edges, and a dry one to cover any mishaps around the carving board.

No matter how informal or relaxed one's style of living, there is a certain ritual to carving and serving that communicates itself from the carver to his or her guests or family, and heightens their appreciation of each other, and of the food they are sharing.

At home, when my wife has a day off in the city, my greatest pleasure is to prepare a little dinner for myself and the children, a *vitello*, perhaps, with prosciutto and cheese, or a roast chicken cooked on the barbeque after the coals have turned to hot ash. When it is ready, I light the candles and my daughter pours the wine and we sit down to enjoy ourselves. A friend who dropped in unexpectedly one evening said in astonishment, "You do all this just for your kids?" All I could think of to say was "And why not?"

Carving Fowl

Roast Chicken

Skillfully done, the carving of a whole chicken is a lovely sight to watch, and it should always be done at the table. In Stresa, at the hotel school I attended in my late teens, we were taught, among other things such as management, reception and food preparation, to carve and reassemble a chicken at tableside with the loving care usually reserved for a work of art. A few months after graduation, on my first job at an hotel in Locarno, I discovered that the Swiss had their own way with chicken. It was not a pretty sight. In the kitchen, the chef would use a cleaver to "carve" the bird. Mopping his brow with a potholder in one hand, he would toss two macerated hunks of chicken on a serving plate with the other, add a spoonful of peas and a ladleful of gravy and thrust the plate at me. In rage and humiliation, I had to bring this offering to the table. Had I been older and more experienced, or needed the job less, I would have left at once. The least I could do was vow never again to take a job where the food was "served" from the kitchen.

As you develop your own skill in carving a chicken, keep in mind that it is a delicate bird. If your knife is sharp enough it is never necessary to hack or slash. The slightest touch from a well-honed blade will separate the skin, and the gentlest probing with the tip of the knife will find the joint you wish to cut. A perfect filet from the breast will fall away with only a whisper from the edge of your knife blade. Keep calm, don't rush, and the bird will return your respect.

In ordering a chicken, it helps to know that one weighing 3 pounds will serve 4 people.

What You Will Need: Your grandmother's nicest china platter (20"x10") or a similar-size platter of stainless steel or silver; a wooden board of approximately the same size on which to do the carving. Never carve *anything* on either silver or stainless steel; it not only scars the surface but it makes an ugly noise. You will also need an ordinary table fork and a knife 8–10" long.

Carving: Present the bird on the platter, its breast facing the guests, garnished with parsley or watercress.

If you are going to serve the carved pieces from the serving platter and not directly onto individual plates, transfer the garnish to one end of the platter.

Place the knife blade in one opening of the chicken cavity and the fork in the other, and remove the chicken to the board, its feet facing the carver **(1).** Tilt the chicken to drain any juices. With the tip of your knife, remove any trussing strings.

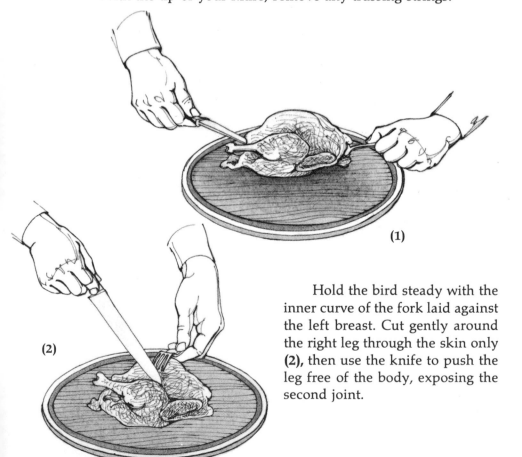

(1)

(2)

Hold the bird steady with the inner curve of the fork laid against the left breast. Cut gently around the right leg through the skin only **(2)**, then use the knife to push the leg free of the body, exposing the second joint.

Cut through the joint **(3)**.

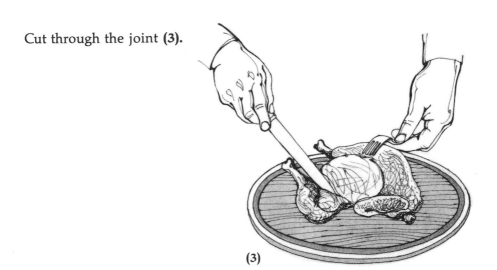

(3)

Turn the leg over and feel for the knee joint with the tip of the knife. Cut through it, dividing the thigh from the drumstick **(4)**.

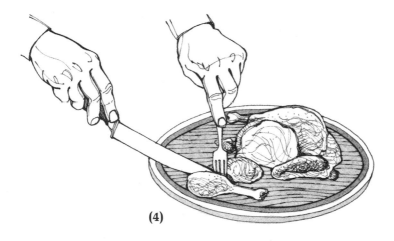

(4)

Carve the left leg in the same way. However, on this side use the fork instead of the knife to push the leg away from the body.

Transfer these 4 pieces back to the serving platter or to serving plates. Although the thigh and the drumstick are both dark meat, traditionally the thigh is presented to the ladies and the drumstick reserved for the men.

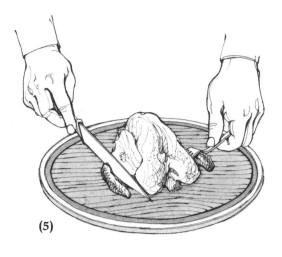

Remove the wings as you did the legs. Cut each wing in two at the joint **(5)**.

(5)

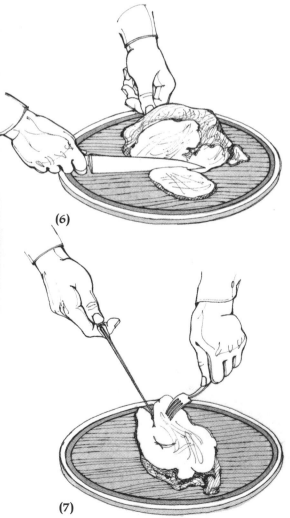

(6)

(7)

Turn the bird so the front faces the carver. Pierce the carcass with the fork just above the left wing bone. Place the knife halfway between the wishbone and the right breast. Slice down toward the wing joint and through it to the carving board to make the first breast filet **(6)**.

Pull the fork out a little so it will not interfere with the passage of the knife blade, and repeat on the left side.

Lay the chicken flat and insert the knife above the wing bone, separating the wishbone **(7)**.

Lift the chicken with the fork so that it is upright on its breast. Rest the knife in the incision through the wishbone.

With the knife, gently force down the central portion of breast meat **(8)**.

(8)

Now you will see the best part of the chicken: two little rounds of meat lying on either side of the lower back. These we call the "oysters." Remove them with the tip of the knife and set them aside **(9).** Cut the filet of breast meat in half lengthwise.

(9)

Now for the "pope's nose," which customarily, in my family at least, garnishes the plate of the host. Rest the flat of the knife against the top of the pope's nose and gently but firmly pull the carcass away **(10).** Some of the skin will come along with the nose—a delicious dividend for the carver.

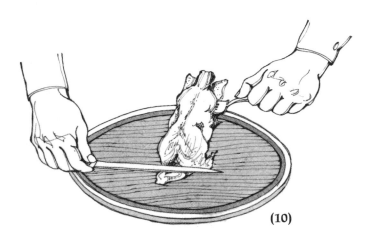

(10)

Serving: If you have arranged the meat on individual serving plates while you were carving, garnish these with the watercress or parsley from the serving platter. If not, set the chicken pieces on the platter and rearrange the garnish. Notice that the pieces are laid out on the platter in the same way they are arranged on the chicken. You can either serve from the platter or let your guests help themselves.

Roast Turkey
(or Capon)

Americans are still inclined to approach a turkey with a reverence that in Italy is reserved for a whole roast pig. Even if the man in the family isn't used to doing the day-to-day carving, he takes his place at the carving board on Thanksgiving when the turkey is brought to the table. Some households even have a special platter reserved for it, emblazoned with an image of the bird, which is kept in the back of a cupboard and brought out only at Thanksgiving and sometimes at Christmas. Yet considering how inexpensive turkey is compared to most meats, I'm surprised that it isn't served more often.

Carving a turkey is no more difficult than carving a roast chicken. There is simply more of it to do. The trickiest part of the operation is getting the turkey to the table on a slippery serving platter, and from the platter to carving board. Accidents have been known to happen. If you should have one, remember America's first lady Mrs. Eleanor Roosevelt, who refused to panic when her maid let the turkey slide to the floor. "That's all right, Marie," she's reported to have said, calmly. "Just take it out to the kitchen and bring in the other one."

These days, a fresh-killed turkey is not always easy to find, but it's worth looking for a butcher who can get you one because the flavor is so much better than the frozen kind. When you're buying turkey remember the rule: the bigger the bird the less the flavor. A 12- to 13-pound turkey, without stuffing, will serve 10 people; with stuffing, 12 people. So if you are planning to serve more than 12 people, it is better to buy two smaller turkeys than one big one.

A capon is carved in the same way as a turkey, except that the wings are removed with ½" of breast meat and served along with the rest of the bird. (We don't serve the turkey wings because they are tough and scrawny.) Instead of slicing down the breast meat on the capon, remove it in filets as with roast chicken. The only difference is that you will get two instead of one filet on each side of the breast.

Before you begin to carve your turkey, let it rest on the serving platter for half an hour after you take it out of the oven. Once you've begun the carving don't feel you must rush; the meat will keep warm another 20 or 25 minutes. And the hot giblet gravy you will be serving on top of the meat will also help to keep it warm.

What You Will Need: Your best china, silver or stainless steel serving platter, of a size to fit the bird with plenty of room to spare; a wooden carving board of the same size; a tablespoon or serving spoon for the stuffing; a table fork, a firm 10" chopping knife and a 12–14" slicing knife.

Carving: Bring your beautifully browned bird on the platter to the table for all to admire. Use the fork and the serving spoon to transfer it to the carving board. Place the bird with the legs facing the carver **(1).**

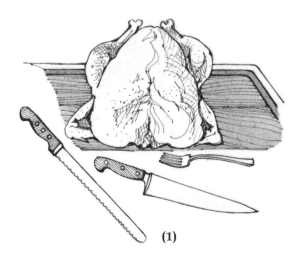

(1)

Steady the bird with the inside of the fork resting on the surface of the left breast. With the chopping knife, cut through the skin between the right leg and the body. Use the flat of the blade **(2)** to force the leg away from the body and look for the leg joint. Going just under the pope's nose, cut through the leg joint all the way to the board, separating the leg.

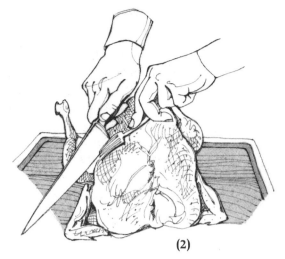

(2)

With the knee of the leg facing the carver, cut between the thigh and the drumstick until you can feel the knee joint. Insert the tip of the knife into the joint and separate the thigh from the drumstick **(3).**

Slice away the meat on both sides of the upper joint **(4).** Cut it across the grain into strips about 1″ wide. Set the bone aside to use with the drumsticks, wings and carcass for soup.

Put the meat aside on the serving platter.

Remove the second leg and carve it as you did the first. Put the slices aside with the rest of the dark meat. Between the thigh and the drumstick you will find that you have enough dark meat for five people.

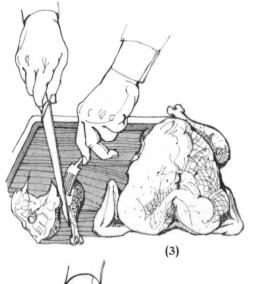

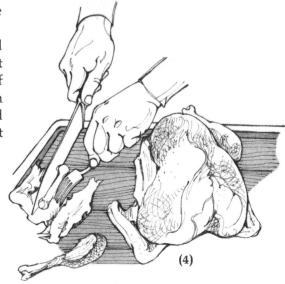

(3)

(4)

Use the slicing knife to make an incision just above the right wing bone, and carry it over the carcass to the wishbone **(5)**. Now begin cutting slices $\frac{1}{8}''$ thick across the breast to the incision **(6)**. After each cut move your knife $\frac{1}{8}''$ up so the slices will all have the same thickness. Keep going until you reach the breastbone. Put the slices aside on the serving platter. Remember to overlap them a bit to help keep them warm and moist.

Repeat on the left side of the breast, turning the carcass slightly. Arrange the slices with the white meat you cut earlier.

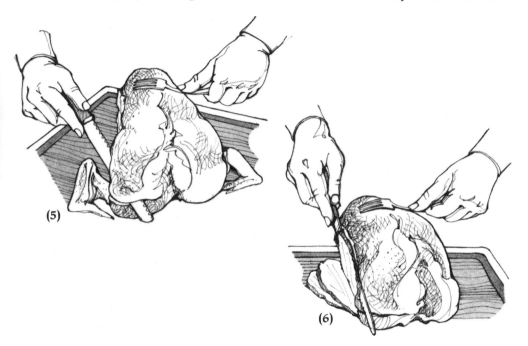

(5)

(6)

Serving: Place 2 pieces of dark meat on each plate, tuck in a bit of the stuffing, and cover the whole thing with three nice-looking pieces of white meat. Place the meat closest to the guest on the plate, and the vegetables on the opposite side. Serve with giblet gravy and garnish with cranberry sauce.

Long Island Duck
(or Goose)

It may surprise you that a 4- to 4½-pound dressed duck will serve only 3 people. That is because 30 to 35 percent of its weight is fat, which is lost in the cooking. So, for 6 people you should order a pair of ducks.

A goose is carved in the same way as a duck. The only difference is that you make an additional filet on each side of the breast. A dressed goose weighing 6 to 8 pounds is enough for 4 people.

What You Will Need: A 20x14″ serving platter and a carving board of about the same size; a table fork; and a firm carving knife 8″ long. Don't bother with poultry shears, even if you happen to have them. A knife does the same job just as effectively, and it's a nuisance to have more cutlery around the carving board than you actually need.

Carving: Bring the ducks on the platter to the table. With the fork and the flat side of the knife blade, remove one of the birds to the carving board, arranged so that the legs are pointing toward the carver.

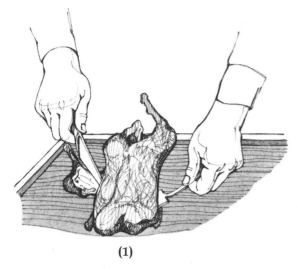

(1)

Rest the fork against the left wing bone. With the knife, make an incision through the skin around the right leg. Press the blade to the right, forcing the leg away from the body and exposing the leg joint. Now cut through the leg joint to the board, separating it from the body (1). Scrape away any fat from the leg. But, since nobody can get rid of all the excess duck fat, don't be too concerned if you can't.

Holding the fork in the same position, repeat the previous step on the left side of the duck.

Now find the joint with the tip of your knife and separate each drumstick from the thigh (2).

(2)

Turn the bird about 45° to the right. With the point of the knife, make an incision along the top of the breast. Follow the angle of the wishbone until you reach the wing bone. Now feel with the point of the knife for the wing joint **(3).** Bring down the blade to cut through the wing joint to the board. Press the knife away from the body, separating wing and breast in one piece **(4).** Use the knife to scrap away all the fat you can.

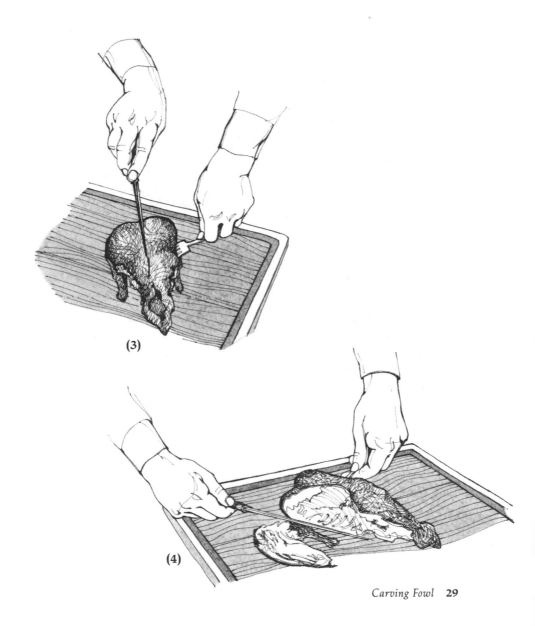

(3)

(4)

Repeat this step on the left side of the bird.

With the knife, separate the wings from the breast.

Rest the outer curve of the fork on the floor of the inner carcass. Now, using the knife, go under the wishbone and push it free of the carcass (5). Even if there are no children at the table, it is fun to give it to one of the guests to make a wish.

Repeat with the other duck as you did with the first.

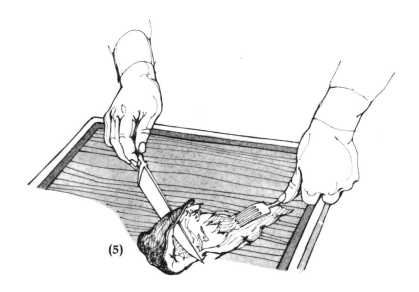

(5)

Serving: Arrange the drumsticks and wing bones at one end of the platter with the thighs. Lay the breasts on top and add the wishbone to make an attractive presentation. As always, you are presenting the bird in much the same way as it was before carving.

Quail

Two fresh 4- to 5-ounce quail will serve one person. A single bird is enough for one person if you're planning another meat course to follow. When buying quail, look to see whether the feet have been removed. If they have, the bird very likely has been frozen, and you don't want it. A frozen bird of such a small size is always tough and flavorless—a far cry from the quail we used to trap as children in the fields behind our house in Mantua.

Should you be wondering why we bother to carve such a tiny bird at all, the reason is that it makes it easier to eat. It also helps the sauce to get to all parts of the bird and improves its flavor.

What You Will Need: A table fork and a sharp carving knife 8–10″ long; a serving platter of a size to fit the number of birds you are serving; and a carving board of approximately the same size.

Carving: Present the birds to your guests with the breast toward them.

Use the inside of the fork and the flat side of the knife blade to transfer the quail to the carving board. Place it on its back, with the legs facing the carver.

Rest the inside of the fork over the left wing, being careful not to pierce the breast. With the knife, make an incision between the right leg and the body. Now press the leg away from the body without removing it **(1).**

(1)

Make an incision on either side of the breast **(2).** In this case, we are not cutting up the bird, merely opening it up.

Repeat on the left side of the quail.

Serving: Return the birds to the serving platter, or to individual serving plates, with a bit of the garnish. Arrange them with the feet pointing toward the center of the platter or plate. Cover with a sauce **(3).**

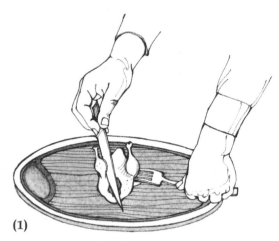

(2)

(3)

Baby Pheasant
(or Cornish Hen or Squab)

For this bird, you will probably have to go to one of the fancier butcher shops rather than to the supermarket. Ask for a young female pheasant, one that has been farm-raised. As you know, the kind your hunting friends bring you have been running in the woods, and with all that unsupervised exercise they are impossibly tough.

A bird weighing from $1\frac{1}{2}$ to $1\frac{3}{4}$ pounds before cleaning will serve 2 people. In buying Cornish hen or squab, plan on one per person.

What You Will Need: A serving platter that will fit the number of birds you are serving, with room to spare; a wooden carving board of approximately the same size; a table fork and a carving knife 8–10″ long.

Carving: Bring the bird or birds to the table on the platter, garnished with watercress. With the fork and the flat side of the knife blade, carefully remove the pheasant from the serving platter to the board. Place it so that the legs are facing the carver.

Rest the inside of the fork on the left wing. Make an incision with the knife on the right side through the skin that lies between the leg and the body. Bring the knife down until you have exposed the leg joint. Now cut through the joint and push the leg free of the body **(1).**

Separate the drumstick from the thigh at the knee joint **(2).** If you are serving a bird of this size as one portion, it is not customary to serve the drumsticks. Save them with the carcass for soup.

Repeat as before on the left side of the bird. Turn the legs over and rest them on the board.

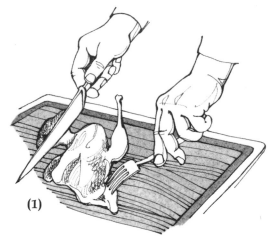

Make an incision with the knife just above the right wing bone. Now cut all the way around to, but not through, the back of the carcass **(3).** Cut along the backbone to free the breast. Use the point of your knife and the fork to remove the breast, leaving the wing bone. We don't serve the wing because, as with all birds that fly, it is tough and meatless.

Without removing the fork, make an incision just to the left of the wishbone. Carry the cut as before all the way around to, but not through, the back of the carcass. Then cut along the backbone to free the second breast **(4).** Remove the fork and use it with the tip of the knife to take away the breast meat.

(4)

Serving: Arrange the drumstick and second joint at angles on the platter or serving plate. Cover them cannily with the breast meat. As always, you want to put the most attractive pieces on top to hide the ones that don't look as well. Add whatever vegetable you are serving, unless it is one with a creamy sauce. In this case, you'll want to serve it separately.

Carving Beef

Standing Rib Roast

Few cuts can match the grandeur of a standing rib roast. At the Café Royal in London, where I was in charge of the cold meats buffet, doing the carving at tableside, this imposing cut was the most popular with the guests who came to dine after the theater in the crimson damask dining room.

For all its imposing character, this cut is very simple to carve—as long as you remember to ask the butcher to remove the shin bone that lies at the base of the meat. This way, you will have no difficulty in freeing the ribs. In ordering, keep in mind that a 6-rib roast will serve 6 people with the ribs; without the ribs, 10 people.

What You Will Need: A large serving platter of china, silver or stainless steel; a carving board big enough to accommodate the roast and still leave plenty of room for your work; a fork; and a firm serrated slicing knife, 16" long. Also, a good-looking kitchen towel or one of your second-best napkins to hold the roast.

Carving (with ribs): Present the roast alone on the platter. A cut with such self-confidence needs no garnish. Using the napkin or towel, grasp the roast by the first rib and transfer it from the serving platter to the carving board. Rest it on its base, with the ribs facing the carver **(1).**

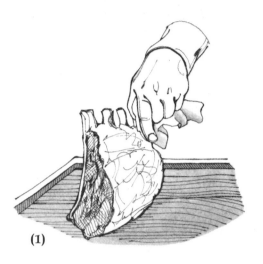

(1)

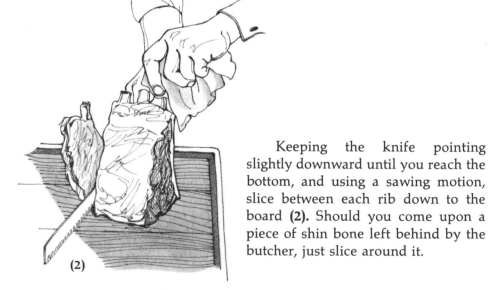

(2)

Keeping the knife pointing slightly downward until you reach the bottom, and using a sawing motion, slice between each rib down to the board **(2).** Should you come upon a piece of shin bone left behind by the butcher, just slice around it.

Serving: To keep the board from getting too crowded, serve as you go: one rib to each guest on a serving plate, with whatever vegetable you have chosen.

Carving (without ribs): Place the roast on the board with the fat side to the right of the carver.

Grasp the first rib in the napkin to steady the roast **(3).** Now cut close to the bone all the way down to the board, removing the ribs and a small amount of fat covering **(4).**

Trim off the crispy fat portions and set them aside.

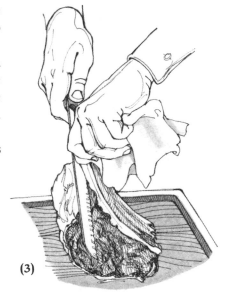

(3)

(4)

Place the roast on its cut side. Gently rest the fork on top of it. With the knife, make slices ¼″ thick across the grain **(5).** Cut them straight down to the board as you would a loaf of bread.

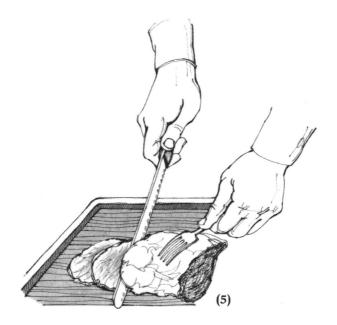

(5)

Serving: Serve 2 slices to each person, with a bit of the crispy fat. Only serve the outside slices to the guests who ask for them. It's not for you to ask because there are not that many people these days who care for well-done meat, and you don't want to force those outside pieces on your friends.

Filet of Beef

In buying this cut keep in mind that a filet mignon 22–24" long (4½ to 5 pounds), with the fat removed, will serve no more than 8 people. This is because you will be using only the first 15–16" of the meat, measuring from the broadest point of the filet.

In preparing the filet for cooking, cut off the lower, skinnier part below the dividing line described above and put it in the refrigerator for use in other dishes such as boeuf bourguignonne or a stroganoff. Before cooking, also cut off the 2–2½" of meat that lie on the side at the head of the filet. This is the "chateaubriand." Put this, too, in the refrigerator and serve it another time for an intimate little dinner for two (see page 45).

What You Will Need: A serving platter large enough to hold the sliced beef and the garnish that goes with it; a carving board of equal size; a table fork; and a firm 8" knife.

Carving: Present the filet on the serving platter, garnished with watercress or parsley. Use the fork and the flat of the knife blade to transfer it to the carving board.

Hold the filet steady with the underside of the fork resting gently on the top surface of the meat. Begin at the broadest end, and keeping the blade of your knife slightly tilted, carve across the grain **(1).** Make slices $\frac{1}{4}$–$\frac{1}{2}''$ thick. Instead of letting these slices fall as they may, keep them stacked closely together on one side of your carving board as you cut them. This way, they will stay warm and juicy.

(1)

Serving: Arrange the slices attractively on the serving platter with the garnish, or put them on individual plates with a bit of the garnish.

Chateaubriand

This delicious cut comes to you as part of a filet of beef. Before cooking the filet, cut off the 2–2½″ of meat, averaging 15 ounces, that lies to the side of the head. This is the "chateaubriand." A 15-ounce piece will serve 2 people.

Before roasting the chateaubriand, wrap it in a dishtowel and flatten it with the side of a cleaver to give it a thinner, rounder shape.

What You Will Need: A small serving platter; a carving board large enough to accommodate the sliced meat; a fork; and a firm 16″ knife.

Carving: Bring the beef to the table on the platter, garnished with watercress. Use the outside curve of the fork and the flat side of the knife to transfer it to the carving board.

Steady the cut with the underside of the fork. With the knife at a 75° angle, carve across the grain in slices ¼–½″ thick.

Serving: Divide the slices onto 2 plates and add some of the watercress.

Double Steak

Steak is still the number-one choice of Americans dining out in restaurants at night. And when they order steak they mean just that—no mustard, which a European would ask for; no sauces, not even a nice Béarnaise. I am constantly amazed at such Spartan taste.

In ordering a double steak, count on a 16- to 18-ounce piece of beef to serve 2 people.

What You Will Need: A china, silver or stainless steel serving platter; a carving board large enough to accommodate the steak; a fork; and a firm knife 16″ long.

Carving: Bring the steak to the table on the platter, garnished with watercress. Use the fork and the flat of the knife to transfer it to the carving board.

Place the underside of the fork lightly on the surface of the steak to steady it. With the knife, carve across the grain, keeping the blade slightly tilted, to make slices ¼-½″ thick **(1)**. As you go, stack them closely together at one end of the board to keep them moist and warm.

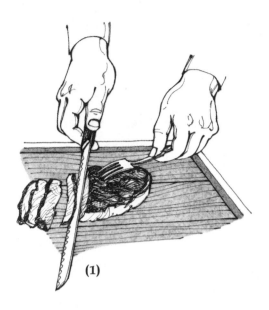

(1)

Serving: Place the slices on a serving platter, add some of the garnish, and spoon some of the delicious juices over each serving.

T-bone Steak

This steak is particularly good because of the difference in texture and flavor between the sirloin and the tenderloin. If you don't use the bone for soup, it will make a *cordon bleu* dinner for your dog. A 12-ounce steak will serve 2 people and one dog.

What You Will Need: A china, silver or stainless steel serving platter large enough to fit the steak and the garnish; a fork; and a firm 8″ knife.

Carving: Bring the steak to the table on the platter, garnished with watercress and perhaps a few cherry tomatoes. Use the fork and the flat of the knife to transfer it to the carving board.

Place the meat flat on the board and steady it with the underside of the fork. With the tip of the knife, slice close to the bone that forms the stem of the "T," on both sides **(1).**

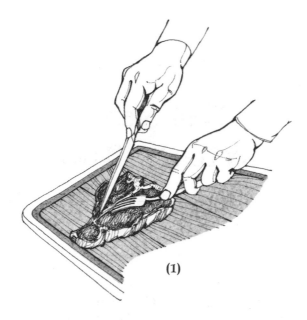

(1)

Now cut across each section beneath the top of the "T," again working close to the bone.

Carve the freed sections of meat across the grain, in slices ½–¼" thick. As you go, stack them closely together at one end of the board to keep them warm and juicy.

Serving: Place the slices on a serving platter, add a handful of watercress, and spoon the juices over the meat.

Flank Steak
(or London Broil)

The flank steak makes a good family or company meal, especially when your geography and climate make it possible to use an outdoor grill. Very often the trouble with London Broil, when it is served at home, is that people slice it like a loaf of bread, straight up and down. The result is something that tastes—not like bread, but not like fine beef either. With the method we've shown below you get a good tender slice.

In ordering flank steak, allow ½ pound for one serving.

What You Will Need: A china, silver or stainless steel serving platter; a carving board large enough to fit the steak and the slices you will be cutting; a fork; and a firm 16″ knife.

Carving: Rest the outside curve of the fork on the meat to steady it. Cutting across the grain, make your first slice almost horizontal along the top surface of the steak **(1).**

(1)

Now switch your knife blade to an angle of about 45° and continue slicing along the top, making the slices as thin as possible. Move the knife along about ⅛″ each time you make a cut so that the slices are all the same size **(2).**

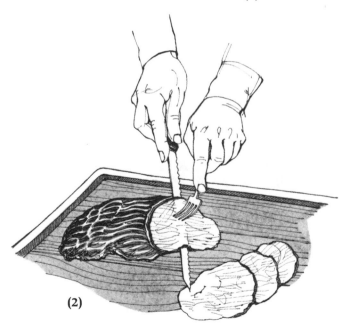

(2)

Serving: Serve 4 or 5 slices to each person.

Brisket

Brisket is the hard-working part of the beef, lying just above the shank. It has supported a lot of running around before it reaches your table, so you can't expect it to be very tender. Long slow cooking in a broth or other liquid will do a lot to make it more so, but equally important is the way you carve it.

Look first for the direction of the grain, and then cut across it. If you cut with the grain, you'll get tough, stringy pieces that few would care to eat. Also, the thinner the slice, the more tender the meat, so make your slices as thin as possible.

As little as a 3-pound piece of brisket will serve 6 people. This is because it is almost never served alone. Somehow, its flavor seems to improve in the company of other meats, such as poached chicken and a spicy sausage.

What You Will Need: A serving platter big enough to accommodate the sliced brisket and whatever other meats and vegetables you will be serving with it; a wooden carving board on which to carve it comfortably (you don't want pieces falling over the side and ruining a nice tablecloth); a table fork; and a sharp 10–12″ slicing knife.

Carving: Transfer the roast from the platter to the carving board, fat side up, with the tip to the right of the carver.

Begin cutting at the tip, keeping your knife at a slight angle and making the slices as thin as possible **(1).**

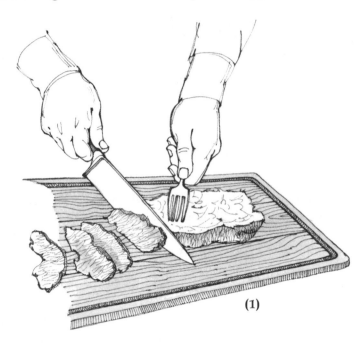

(1)

Serving: Arrange the slices attractively on the serving platter along with the other meats and a vegetable or two in season **(2).**

(2)

Corned Beef

Corned beef is not a dish that you are likely to serve at a dinner party or one that you will find on the menu in a fine restaurant. It is more often served at home to the family. A helpful thing to know about carving corned beef is that its interest depends on the contrast between the fat part and the lean. So forget about Jack Spratt and his wife and make sure that each person gets some of each.

Again, because this is a less tender cut of beef, look for the grain and make certain that you cut across, not with it. (This is tricky because the grain of corned beef changes from point to point.) Otherwise the meat will be so tough and stringy that even the youngest and hungriest in the family is likely to complain.

What You Will Need: A serving platter large enough to accommodate the beef as well as the vegetable you are serving with it; a good-sized carving board; a table fork; and a 8–10" slicing knife.

Carving: Place the beef, fat side up, on the carving board, with the tip to the right of the carver. Take the time before you begin to look at the direction of the grain. If you're not sure how it runs, take off a thin slice or two just to be certain.

Beginning at the tip, make ¼″ slices across the grain **(1)**. Now turn the meat as the grain changes to make sure you're always cutting across the grain. Make more slices of both fat and lean.

(1)

Serving: Arrange the slices attractively in the center of the platter and surround them with a vegetable.

Salami
(or other hard sausage)

I have always had a special place in my heart for salami. It was the first meat that I learned to carve, at the age of eleven, not tableside, but in a corner of the family restaurant under the watchful eye of my father. I can still remember the satisfaction I felt at the sound and feel of the skin as I peeled it away from the sausage and sniffed the glorious aroma of garlic.

What You Will Need: A wooden carving board; a short, fairly flexible slicing knife; and a nice-looking kitchen towel to grasp the end of the sausage.

Carving: In the kitchen, remove the skin of the sausage up to the point where you expect to finish carving. Here, in private, you can do this with your fingers.

Present the salami at the table on the carving board. Use the towel to steady the end of the sausage and begin cutting across the meat at a slight angle, making the slices as thin as possible **(1).** Sliced at an angle, the pieces not only look more attractive, but you gain one-third more meat than if you cut straight down. This way, there is also less solid fat in each slice.

(1)

Serving: Arrange the sausage in overlapping slices on a serving platter with other appetizers, and garnish with parsley **(2)**.

(2)

Carving Lamb

Leg of Lamb

In ordering lamb, you have to consider the weight of the bone as well as the weight lost in cooking. For instance, a leg weighing 10 pounds has from 2½ to 3 pounds of bone and will lose another pound in the course of the cooking. (Make sure not to overcook the lamb. It should not be more than medium.) This will leave 6 pounds of lamb, enough to serve 10 to 12 people. If you are serving more than that number of guests, order two legs rather than one weighing more than 10 pounds. Anything larger than that is likely to belong to an elderly beast and will certainly taste that way.

Frozen lamb from New Zealand is widely available in supermarkets, and its source of origin is marked by law. My advice is to avoid it. It is likely to be quite fat, and you can never be sure of its freshness at the time of freezing. In fact, I would avoid all frozen lamb; it simply does not compare in flavor with the fresh. One way of telling whether American lamb has been frozen is to look at the grain of the meat. If it is pale, it's been frozen.

What You Will Need: A table fork; a firm slicing knife, 12–14" long; and an attractive dishtowel to hold the roast. Also, a serving platter large enough to fit the lamb; and a carving board of equal size.

Carving: Allow the lamb to rest on the serving platter for 10 to 15 minutes after you take it out of the oven. Then present it with the smooth side facing your guests.

With a little help from the dishtowel wrapped around the end of the leg bone, transfer the meat to the carving board. Place it so that it rests on its meatier side.

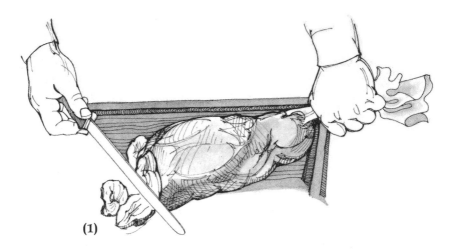

(1)

At the top of the leg begin slicing at a bit of an angle, making slices about ⅛″ thick **(1)**. Keep going until you reach the round knob of the bone. These slices will be fewer and less perfect than the ones you will be cutting later. Set them at one end of the board where they will not be in the way of your carving.

Now rest the roast on its smooth side. Begin slicing at the meatiest point on the inside of the leg, above and to the right of the small round bone. Move your knife along ⅛″ at a time to get slices of uniform thickness, and be sure that your cuts go all the way down to the bone **(2)**.

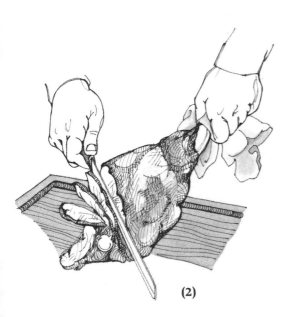

(2)

Let the slices fall until you have cut as many as you need, then cut across the bottom to release them **(3).** Set them aside with the slices cut earlier.

Turn the leg smooth side up and repeat as above.

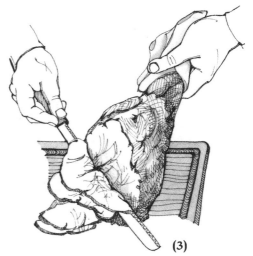

(3)

The final stage of carving is the rich-tasting collar of meat around the leg bone. Some people consider this the very best part of the leg. Cut about 3″ below the collar around the bone to free it **(4).** Now slice the collar into smaller pieces across the grain.

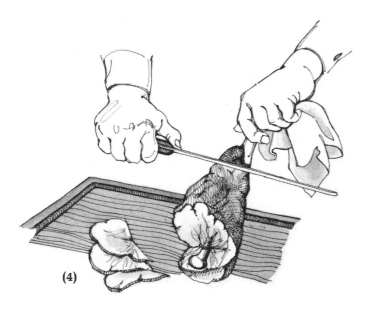

(4)

Serving: Serve each guest with slices from both sides of the leg and a bit of the collar, garnished with roast potatoes and a green vegetable in season.

Saddle of Lamb

This versatile cut, with its delicious variety of textures, was one that appeared daily in a New York restaurant, the name of which we won't mention. Three different roasts were prepared each morning and brought on a buffet cart to the table. It was part of my job there as the captain to carve them to order. I tell this story to illustrate that even in the finest restaurants a captain and a whole saddle of lamb are subject to accident.

One day, during a crowded lunchtime, the young "commis de rang," the busboy, who helped me with the serving reached down to retrieve the napkin of one of the guests. As he stood up to hand it to her, he accidentally knocked against my arm. Its point deep in the roast, the knife that I held in my hand was wrenched to one side, and the saddle slid from the platter. It was already well on its way to the floor when a quick jerk of my knee, worthy of the smoothest karate move, brought it back to the level of the serving table. With our backs to the guests, my assistant and I hastily reassembled it on the platter, as the lady with the lost napkin murmured her thanks.

If you are still prepared to serve a saddle of lamb, keep in mind that a whole saddle will serve 6 people. Ask the butcher to tie the meat, without cutting off the flaps (or skirts).

What You Will Need: A warm, good-sized serving platter; a carving board at least twice the size of the roast; an 11" slicing knife; and a table fork.

Carving: Transfer the meat from the serving platter to the carving board, saddle side up. Rest the inner curve of the fork on the upper surface of the roast to steady it. Remove the string with the point of the knife **(1).** Tip the roast as necessary to get at all the string on the underside.

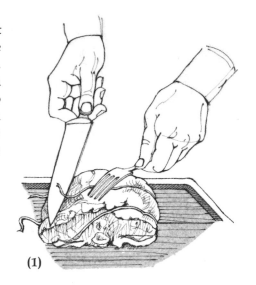

(1)

Turn the roast saddle side down. Lay open the flaps on either side. Now cut them away from the body of the roast **(2).** Also cut out the two mignons on either side of the center bone.

(2)

Cut the skirts at a slight angle across the grain in strips about ½″ thick **(3)**. Set them aside in the center of the serving platter.

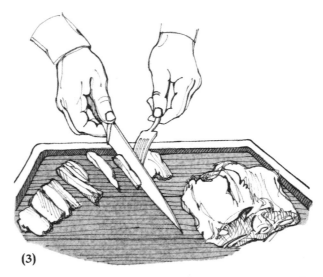

(3)

Return the roast to its original position, saddle side up, and the stem of the flat T-bone that lies between the loin and the tenderloin facing the carver. Take the fork and pierce it lightly just to the left side of the center bone. Now insert the knife along the right side of the center bone **(4)**. Cutting as close to the bone as possible, bring the blade all the way down to the short ribs.

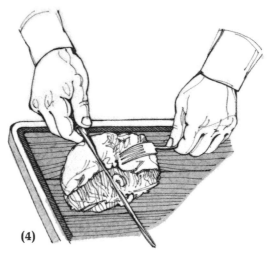

(4)

Remove the knife. Starting at the outside edge of the loin, and holding your knife flat, begin to cut wide slices $\frac{1}{4}''$ thick. Give a little angle to the knife each time you reach the short ribs **(5)**. Stop when you reach the center bone. Arrange the slices on the serving platter in overlapping fashion on top of the skirt strips.

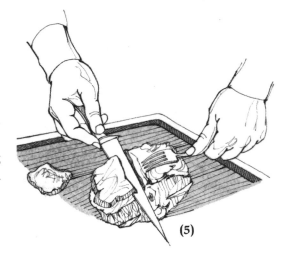

(5)

Reverse the roast from right to left and go ahead in the same way as you did on the other side of the center bone. Arrange these slices in a similar way on the serving platter.

Turn the roast, saddle side down. Keeping your blade at an angle, slice the filets in very thin slices across the grain **(6)**.

Serving: Arrange the slices of tenderloin attractively on top of the other slices already on the platter, and serve with drippings from the roast **(7)**.

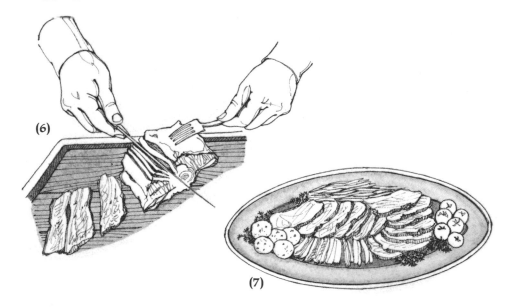

(6)

(7)

Rack of Lamb

An 8-bone rack will serve 3 people. In ordering this cut, remember to have the butcher remove the shin bone. This way, you will avoid having to hack and slash to free the chops from the base of the rack. And do remember to ask him to give you the shin bone. It makes delicious stock.

What You Will Need: A 20"x14" serving platter and a wooden board of approximately the same size; a table knife; and a sturdy knife 8–10" long to cut the meat into chops. If you are using Method II (rack of lamb off the bone), you will need another knife, a short slightly flexible slicer with a blade 10–12" long.

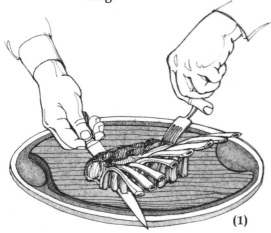

(1)

Carving (Method I): Present the lamb on the platter garnished with watercress and perhaps some tiny green peas or parslied new potatoes. With the fork and the flat side of the knife blade, remove the lamb from the platter to the board. Place it with the bones up and facing away from the carver **(1).**

Lightly pierce the meat with the fork at the left end to steady it. Your first cut will be after the first *two* bones on the right, so as to establish a straight cut. Cut straight down to the board between the second and third rib bones and serve the first two ribs as one chop **(2).**

(2)

Continue cutting between *each* bone, one rib at a time, until you reach the end of the rack **(3).** Be careful not to cut at an angle, but always straight down. Otherwise, you will find yourself winding up with 3 bones and no meat at the end. And this would be a pity, since the last chop on the rack is the tenderest and leanest.

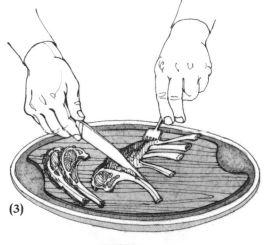

(3)

Serving: Arrange the chops along the outside of the platter, the ends of the bones overlapping as in the illustration **(4).** Replace the vegetables in the center of this arrangement and garnish with watercress.

(4)

Carving Lamb **69**

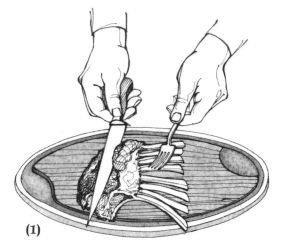

Method II: Lay the rack with the tips of the bones to the left of the carver and flat to the board; rest the fork on the bones.

With the slicer, make an incision where the meat begins on the rack **(1)**.

Now cut all the way down until you reach the bones. Turn the knife at an angle and continue cutting toward the tip of the bones to remove the fatty section, which also includes some meat **(2)**. Slice this into small strips about 1″ wide and set them aside **(3)**.

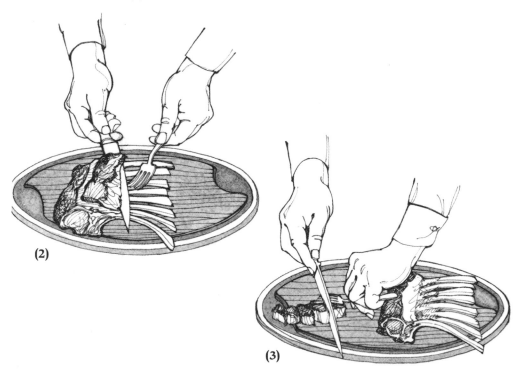

Now place the rack with the bones up. Pierce it lightly with the fork behind the bones to steady it (4). Use the knife to cut the meat that lies in front of the bones, making thin slices all the way down to the board, as if you were carving a roast (5). You should get at least 9 to 10 slices.

(4)

(5)

Now cut through each bone to make chops (6). Of course, they won't be as meaty as the chops in Method I, but they are good to chew on.

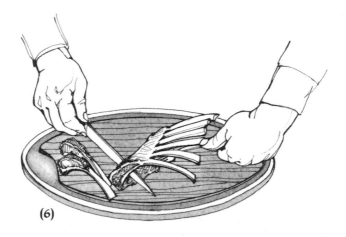

(6)

Serving: Place the chops in crisscross fashion at each end of the platter. Add the meat slices and slivers of fat in an attractive arrangement and rearrange the garnish.

Leg or Shoulder of Baby Lamb

One way you can make sure of getting genuine baby lamb is to know that it is available only in the early spring. At any other time the lamb is bound to be either frozen or a good deal older than the young and tender one you want. The leg should weigh no more than 4 to 4½ pounds, enough to serve 4 people. Try to get a lamb that has been milk-fed only. That is, fed only by its mother, not old enough to graze. These are the ones with the best flavor. You can tell them by the color of the flesh, which is a whitish gray—almost the color of veal—and much lighter than the pink flesh of older lambs.

In Europe, much is made of cooking young lamb out of doors on a spit as a festive dish in celebration of Easter. In my family we would do two or three at a time, beginning in the late afternoon. My brother and I would go out beforehand to gather the cedar wood for the fire. At home, our mother would stuff and truss the meat. Our little sister helped by putting her finger on the strings to hold them as Mother tied the ends. Later, we boys would take turns working the spit. By nightfall, when the fire had turned to coals, the delicious smell of roasting lamb, mingled with rosemary, filled the spring night air. What an agony to wait—and what joy when finally our father would inspect the meat with the tip of his knife and pronounce it ready to eat. If you have qualms about eating such a young creature, try it just once and your conscience will trouble you no more.

In ordering a leg of baby lamb, ask the butcher to remove the bone up to the knee. At home, before you cook it, sprinkle the inside with fresh or dried herbs to your taste, stuff the cavity with bread crumbs and spices, then roll and tie the loose meat. Please note that you can use these instructions in pretty much this form for a lamb shoulder too.

What You Will Need: A serving platter of china, silver or stainless steel large enough to fit the lamb and the garnish; a smaller additional platter; a good-sized carving board that will allow you plenty of room to work; a table fork and a firm, very sharp knife 8–10″ long. You will also need a nice-looking kitchen towel or a paper frill for the leg bone.

Carving: Bring the lamb to the table or sideboard on the serving platter, garnished with a green vegetable and new potatoes, or just plain parsley. Let it rest for 10 to 15 minutes before you present it. Then transfer it to the carving board.

With the fork and the flat of the knife blade, transfer the roast to the carving board, smooth side up. Remove the strings with the tip of your knife and push them aside so they don't get in the way of your work or, heaven forbid, onto someone's plate.

Grasp the leg in the towel with your left hand. Beginning at the broad end of the leg, slice at an angle of 45° in very thin slices **(1).**

(1)

Make sure you are cutting
against the grain. Keep going until
you reach the knee **(2)**.

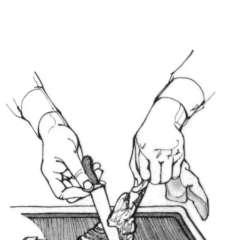

(2)

(3)

Lift the leg by the bone and begin making thin slices the
length of the bone on each side **(3)**. The meat will fall away from
the bone in small, petal-like pieces. There won't be a great
many, but they are delicious and richer in flavor than the slices
you cut earlier.

(4)

Serving: After carving, transfer the pieces to the smaller
serving platter. Arrange them artfully, covering the less attractive pieces with the most perfect **(4)**.

Carving Pork

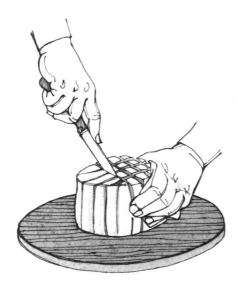

Smoked Ham
(or Fresh Leg of Pork)

There is a lot of confusion around about the word "ham," encouraged by misleading supermarket labels and even some cookbooks. Used correctly, the term applies only to a smoked hind leg of pork. It should not be used for smoked shoulder of pork, which many markets erroneously label "picnic ham." However, smoked ham, fresh leg of pork and smoked shoulder of pork are all carved in the same way. (With the shoulder you will not get the cuts around the shank bone.)

In the United States a smoked ham is generally glazed, scored and studded with cloves. I have seen it, too, very over-decorated with slices of canned pineapple and, God forbid, maraschino cherries perched on toothpicks. In Italy we would serve a hard cured ham, like prosciutto or Parma, covered with a mixture of bread crumbs and herbs and baked in the oven. Like the American turkey, this dish is usually reserved for festivals and other special occasions. The French have a nice way of doing ham; they braise it in a madiera or port wine to give it a fine flavor.

However you cook your ham, and no matter how few people you are serving, it is important to make cuts from both the top and the bottom, as well as around the shank bone. Because of the difference in grain at these points the slices have a very different taste. So give your guests a chance to try some of each.

What You Will Need: Any good, slightly flexible carving knife with a long blade; a large serving platter; and a carving board at least twice the size of the ham. This is one of those cuts where you want to have plenty of room to work. If you happen to have a prosciutto holder, or can afford the extravagance, this springlike device holds the ham in place beautifully. Lacking the holder, you can always steady the roast with your hand and your best-looking kitchen towel.

Carving: In the kitchen, about a half-hour before cooking has finished, remove the skin and glaze the ham. Return the ham to finish baking. Cut the skin you have removed into strips about 1½″ long, deep fry and put them on a plate to serve with the ham. Let the ham rest for 15 or 20 minutes.

Bring the ham to the table on the serving platter and present it to your guests. It will need no further garnish than what you've already added with the glaze.

Transfer the ham to the carving board. Now grasp it by the protruding bone with the folded kitchen towel and turn it bottom side up. Use the knife to take a slice off the bottom to make a nice flat resting surface **(1).**

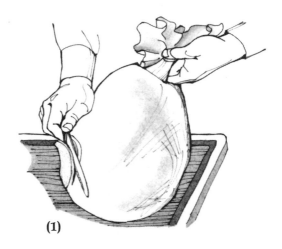

(1)

Turn the ham right side up. Carefully remove the layer of fat along the top surface to the point where you expect to stop carving **(2)**. You may not want to take away all of it, depending on how you feel about fat. Some people think that a thin edge improves the flavor of the ham.

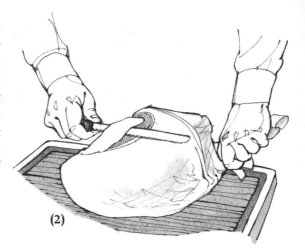

(2)

Now, at the top where you have removed the fat, start cutting thin slices downward at an angle toward the bone. The slant will help you to avoid the bone. The first slices may seem a little fat when you begin, but they will grow leaner as you go further into the meat. Keep going until you have half as many slices as you need per person.

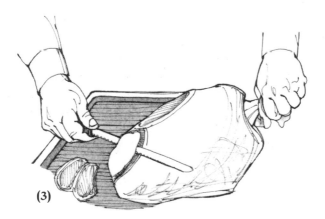

(3)

Start slicing lengthwise along the tip **(3)**. Again, keep going until you have about half as much as you need per serving. The slices will not be as big as the ones you took from the other side, but they will be leaner. This is because the shank bone is closer to where you are cutting.

The next point at which you will be carving is the last and the best. Begin at the end of the shank bone, being careful not to cut your fingers where you are holding it, and cut thin round slices from around the bone (4). You won't get many, not more than 5 or 6, but they are delicious. Now turn the ham over and continue slicing.

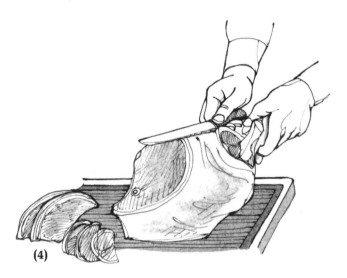

(4)

Serving: Arrange the slices you have cut from the top side of the ham on one side of the serving platter in overlapping fashion. Do the same on the other side of the platter with the slices cut from the bottom. At either end of the platter distribute the slices you have taken from around the shank bone. Arrange the strips of skin, which many people enjoy but don't like to ask for, in the center.

Party Ham
(Rolled Boned Ham)

This is an unusual and attractive way of carving and displaying a ham at a buffet table. When buying, choose a boneless ham weighing from 1½ to 2½ pounds. You won't need more than that if you are serving it with several other dishes at your buffet. Or, you may be serving it as an hors d'oeuvre at a cocktail party.

What You Will Need: A carving board large enough to fit the ham comfortably; a table fork; and a slicing knife 10–12″ long.

Carving: In the kitchen, remove the plastic wrapping and set the ham on its side on the carving board. Use the knife to remove a ¼″ slice at each end **(1)**. If the ham already has a cut face, remove the slice from the butt end only.

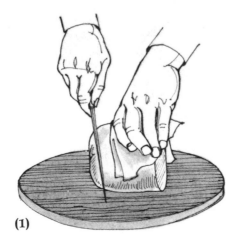

(1)

(2)

Place the ham on one of its cut ends. Make a deep cut at one end of the top surface, straight down, but not quite to the bottom of the ham (2). Move your knife $\frac{1}{2}''$ at a time to repeat the cuts until you are within $\frac{1}{4}''$ of the other edge of the ham.

Turn the ham a half-turn and make cuts at right angles to the previous cuts, in a checkerboard pattern (3). As you continue cutting, the ham will begin to open up slightly to resemble a pineapple. You may want to help along this effect by putting half an apple under the center of the ham.

Transfer the ham to a serving platter and bring it to the buffet table, garnished with watercress and apple slices (4).

(3)

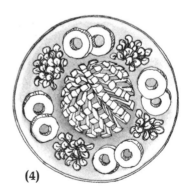

(4)

Serving: Serve with a variety of mustards on the side. Let each guest detach a finger of ham and dip it into the mustard of his choice.

Roast Loin of Pork

In ordering your pork, remember that a 4-pound roast will serve 4 people. Ask the butcher to remove the shin bone for easier carving in either of the methods described below.

What You Will Need: A serving platter; a carving board big enough to accommodate the roast and the pieces you will be carving; a thin, firm 10″ chopping knife; and an ordinary table fork.

Carving (Method I): Present the roast to your guests on the serving platter, surrounded by a vegetable in season. Then use the fork and the flat of the knife blade to transfer it to the carving board. Place it meat side up, resting on the tips of the ribs.

Rest the inner curve of the fork on the surface of the roast. Beginning at the right, use the knife to slice down to the board between each rib to cut nice, even chops **(1).**

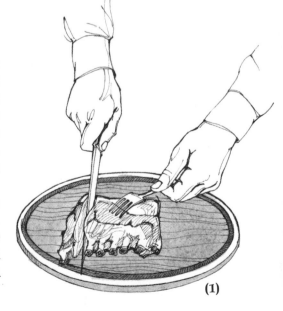

(1)

Serving: Arrange the chops in the center of the serving platter, the tips of the ribs pointing outward toward the rim.

Method II: Transfer the roast to the carving board so that the ribs are at an angle to the carver and resting on the board.

Place the inner curve of the fork against the tip of the ribs. Make an incision with the knife at the beginning of the loin and carry it all the way across the roast and down to the rib bone **(2)**.

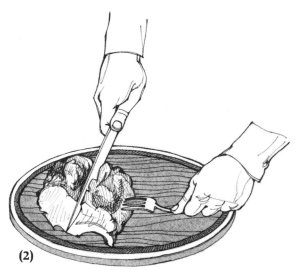

(2)

Insert the fork tines between the rib bones to keep the roast steady. Now press the knife edge along the curve of the ribs, cutting to the board to remove the loin **(3)**.

(3)

From the rib half of the severed roast, remove the upper part, which is the crusty fat **(4)**. Slice it with the grain into small strips about ½″ thick **(5)**. Discard the bony section and arrange the strips on the serving platter.

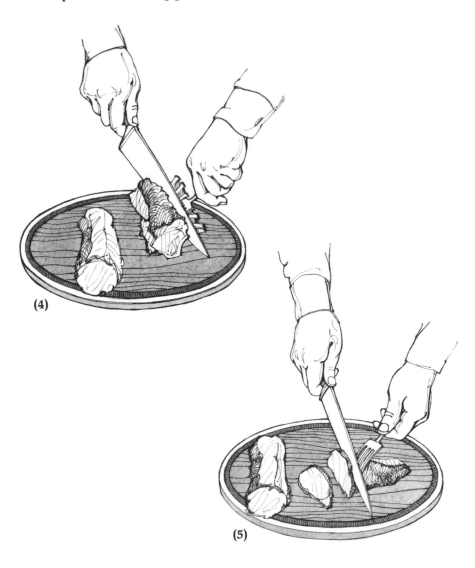

(4)

(5)

Remove the excess fat from the surface of the filet with the knife. Slice the meat into rounds ¼" thick **(6).**

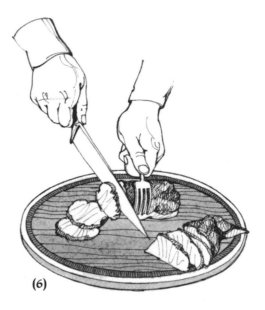

(6)

Serving: On the serving platter place overlapping slices of filet on top of the crusty strips you have arranged earlier. Serve surrounded by the vegetable.

Carving Veal

Roast Breast or Loin of Veal

Because a roast of veal is rather bland, it is best stuffed with herbs to give it extra flavor. When ordering your roast, count on a 3-pound cut to serve between 5 and 6 people. Ask the butcher to bone the meat, but tell him to leave it untied. Don't forget to ask for the bones for making stock. At home, spread the meat on one side with the herbs of your choice, then roll and tie it securely before baking.

What You Will Need: A good-sized serving platter; a wooden carving board; a table fork; and a fairly firm slicing knife with a pointed blade 11″ long.

Carving: Bring the roast to the table on the serving platter, garnished with watercress. Transfer it to the carving board with the help of the fork and the flat of the knife blade and place it on its side. Insert the fork tines under the string and use the point of the knife to cut them (1).

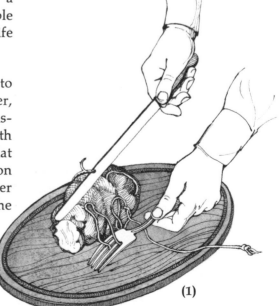

(1)

Roll them aside with the fork, turning the roast as necessary to remove the remaining bits on the underside. As a beginner, you may find this a slightly messy procedure, but it's well worth learning as a deft little prelude to the carving of any rolled roast.

Steady the roast with the inside of the fork laid against the top surface. Using the slicing knife, begin to cut the meat straight down, as you would a loaf of bread **(2).** Keep the tip of the knife pointing downward, and follow through with the rest of the blade to the board. Move your knife along ⅛″ at a time to keep the slices fairly thin and uniform. Cut as many as you need to serve 2 slices per person.

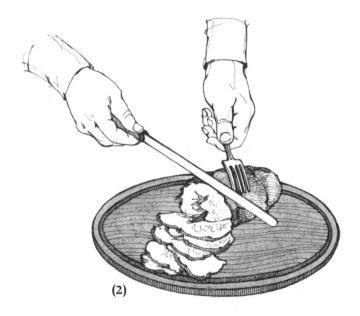

(2)

Serving: Arrange the meat in overlapping slices in the center of the serving platter. Rearrange the watercress, if necessary, and add whatever vegetable you are serving.

Boning Fish
and Lobster

Striped Bass

One of the things I've noticed in my work at the Four Seasons is that recently we've had to increase our supplies of fish. Today, 70 percent of our guests order fish at lunchtime. And bass is a perennial favorite. Four or five years ago, fish would have been a rare request, especially from a male guest, who would more than likely have ordered boeuf bourginonne, or something equally substantial. So it appears that men, too, are watching their waistlines and their cholesterol.

A whole striped bass makes a lovely presentation surrounded by the vegetables from the court bouillon in which it was cooked. The fish should always be presented with the backbone toward the guests. If you are fortunate enough to have dried fennel, it makes a spectacular addition used as a bed for the fish, particularly so when you flambé it. The flaming herb adds a marvelous flavor to the fish.

In ordering bass, remember that a fish weighing 4½ pounds before cleaning will serve 2 people as a main course, 4 as an appetizer.

What You Will Need: A fish fork; an 8–10" palette fish knife; and a sharp boning knife; as well as a plate to take care of the skin and bones. You will also need a china, silver or stainless steel platter large enough to hold the fish and the vegetables—and the fennel bed if you are going to use it. With the exception of smoked salmon, which is carved on a board, fish is always boned on a serving platter.

Boning: *Before cooking* make an incision with the boning knife along the backbone of the fish **(1).** Begin just behind the head and end just above the tail. Remove the strip of bones that lies about ¼″ below the skin. This will make it easier to free the filets after the fish is cooked. If you prefer, you can, of course, have the fish market do this for you when the fish is being cleaned.

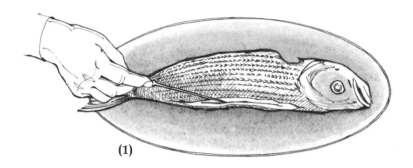

(1)

Bring the fish to the table on the platter after it is cooked. If you are using fennel and want to flambé it, touch it off now and be sure to let the flames die out before you begin your boning! With the palette knife, separate the skin just below the head **(2).**

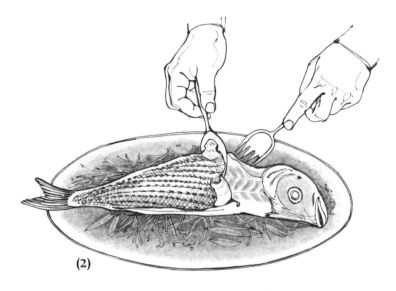

(2)

Now slide the knife under the skin and, with the help of the fork, pull it carefully away from the flesh the entire length of the body **(3).** This is easier to do with a warm fish than a cold one. But if the skin breaks, don't worry. Just keep going from one piece to the next, treating each as a new beginning. Set the skin aside on the side plate, or hide it under the fennel.

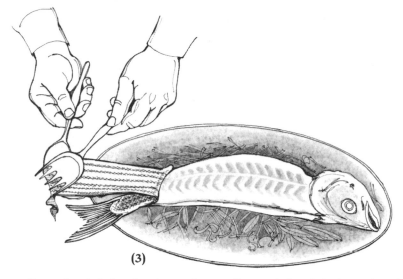

(3)

Run the fish knife along the midline of the fish from head to tail **(4).** Beginning above the midline at the tail, slide the knife under the flesh. It should be resting on the bone.

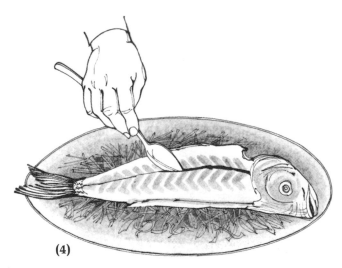

(4)

Now push it along as far as it will go and still support the filet—about halfway up the length of the fish (5). Remove the filet to an individual serving plate.

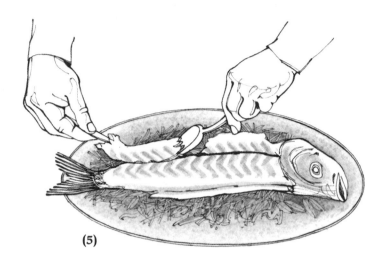

(5)

Repeat below the midline at the tail end, and remove the upper filet (6). Place it on the serving plate with the one taken off earlier.

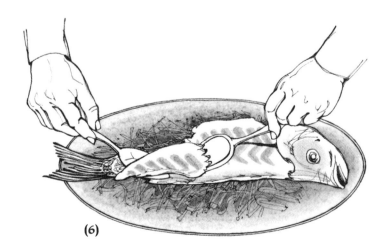

(6)

Working toward the head of the fish, continue pushing the flesh away from the bone with the palette knife to release the third filet **(7)**. (There is no fourth filet because this is where the stomach lies.) What you are doing is not so much cutting as disassembling the fish. Use the knife to support each piece you remove. Steady it on top with the flat of the fork and transfer it carefully to a serving plate **(8)**.

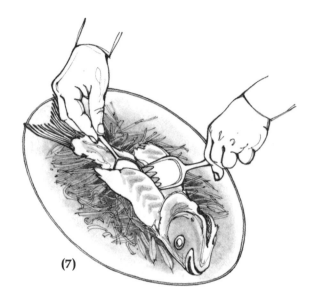

(7)

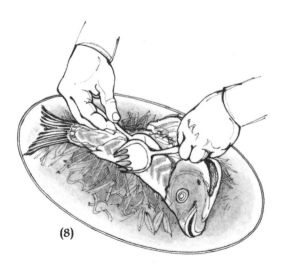

(8)

Now insert the tip of the palette knife under the backbone and push the knife toward the head, freeing the head and the backbone. Push these aside on the platter, toward you. Now you will be able to get at the flesh on the underside of the bass.

With the fork and the palette knife, remove the three filets from the underside of the fish **(9).** Before you put them on serving plates, turn them over to make sure there are no unattractive bits of skin still sticking to them.

(9)

Serving: Serve 2 filets to a person with some of the vegetables and half a lemon. One filet serves one as an appetizer.

Dover Sole

Like caviar or real pearls, there is no substitute for Dover sole. But if you can't find it, or afford it, try Boston sole or flounder or fluke. The boning procedure is the same. However, you will find that with these more ordinary fish the lower filet is much thinner than the upper, and you can't expect to get the same ample serving that you would with Dover sole. Also, since the flesh of flounder tends to crumble, if you are using that fish it is better to do the boning before it is cooked.

In ordering Dover sole, count on 1½ to 1¾ pounds, uncleaned, to serve one person, or 2 people as an appetizer.

What You Will Need: An oval china, silver or stainless steel platter large enough to fit the fish comfortably. The shape of the platter is not that important, but an oval one seems to conform better to the shape of the fish. You will also need a palette fish knife, a fish fork and a separate plate to receive the bones.

Boning: Present the fish on the platter, garnished with parsley. Rest it so that its stomach is facing the carver, and the tail end is to the right of the carver.

(1)

Hold the sole in place with the fork. Now begin to remove the outer edges of the backbone (the first seam of the fish) by pressing against them gently with the palette knife and pushing them aside **(1).** You'll be surprised how easily these small bones come away. Do the same with the outer edges of the lower part, or stomach, of the fish. Remove the bones to the side plate as you work.

Rest the fork on the top surface of the fish to steady it. Insert the tip of the palette knife just to the bone and run it down the center of the fish from head to tail **(2).** Now go back to the head. Slide the knife under the flesh just below the center bone, letting it rest on the bone as you work your way down to the tail to remove the first filet **(3).** Use the fish fork to help free the filet from the bone. Let the filet rest on the platter below the fish.

(2)

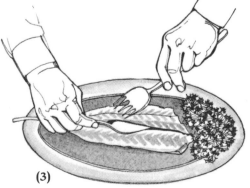

(3)

Remove the second filet that lies above the center bone in the same way **(4).** Arrange it so that it rests above the fish.

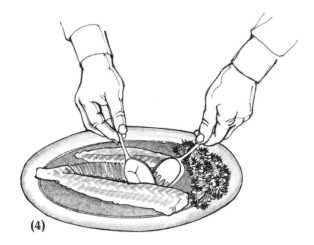

(4)

Hook the fork on to the head end of the backbone and lift it away from the flesh that lies underneath **(5).** In other words, what you are doing is peeling the bone away from the fish. Here, you may need your palette knife to hold down the lower flesh and keep it from coming away with the bone. Give your audience a moment to appreciate your technique; then remove the bone to the side plate.

Use the palette knife to remove the upper and lower filets from the underside of the fish.

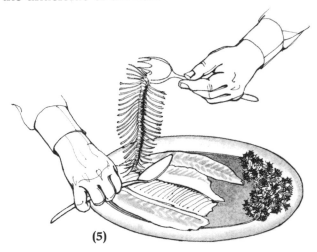

(5)

Serving: Place the 2 bottom filets on a serving plate. Rest the 2 upper filets above them **(6).** Serve with a lemon half and a few sprigs of parsley. Or, serve one top and one bottom filet as an appetizer for one person.

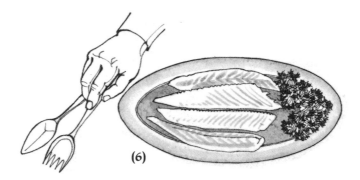

(6)

Poached Trout

Even if you don't encourage your outdoor friends to drop by with a brace of tough wild pheasant, do make a point of asking them to stop in for a drink on the way home from a fishing trip. Fresh-caught trout are not easy to come by, and even though the frozen variety are always available, and are served in many restaurants, they don't taste anything like the ones that were taken from the hook an hour or two before serving. In looking over your friends' catch, keep in mind that a 12-ounce trout will serve one person for dining, 2 as an appetizer. It is best to prepare fish in a poacher on a strainer; this way, you can remove the fish without breaking it.

The important thing to remember in boning trout is that the flesh is more delicate than that of other fish, and the less you handle it the better.

What You Will Need: A fish knife and fork; a silver, china or stainless steel platter large enough to hold the number of trout you are serving.

Boning: Present the fish on the platter, garnished with parsley. The backbone should face your guests, with the head to the right of the carver.

Rest the underside of the fork on the surface of the fish to keep it steady. Now make an incision with the palette knife along the backbone. As you go, use the fork and knife to pull away the large and small fins that lie along it **(1)**.

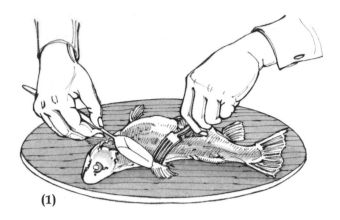

(1)

Remove the two fins that lie along the under edge of the stomach in the same way **(2).** Now push all the fins up near the head of the fish to keep them out of your way.

(2)

With the flat of the knife, go under the skin by the head. Now, with the help of the fork, gently pull the skin back in the direction of the tail (3). It won't all come away in one piece, so expect to go back for the bits you have missed.

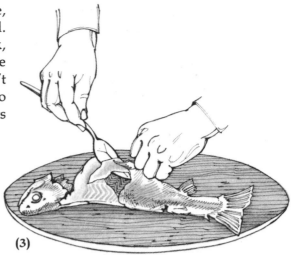

(3)

Make an incision with the knife into the midline of the stomach from the tail to the head. Still using the edge of the knife, gently draw the lower flesh of the stomach toward you (4). Lay it out flat on a plate.

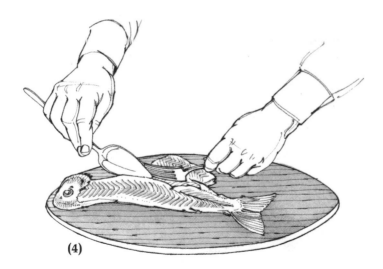

(4)

Repeat with the upper part of the trout, detaching the flesh lightly with the tip of the knife all the way down to the tail **(5)**. Push it away gently from the upper part of the body, and lay it flat on the plate.

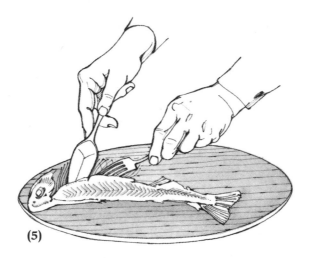

(5)

Insert the fork just under the head to catch the spine bone between the tines **(6)**.

(6)

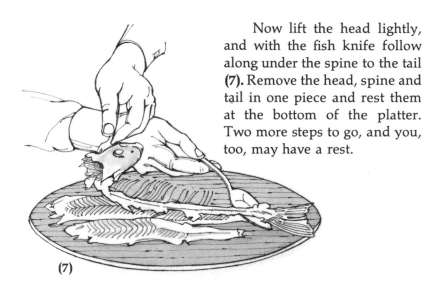

Now lift the head lightly, and with the fish knife follow along under the spine to the tail **(7)**. Remove the head, spine and tail in one piece and rest them at the bottom of the platter. Two more steps to go, and you, too, may have a rest.

(7)

Lift up the lower filet from the skin. Arrange it with the upper filet on the plate **(8).**

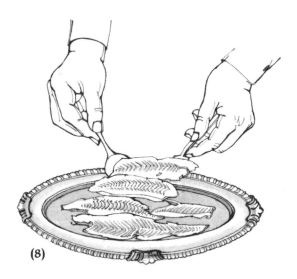

(8)

Insert the tip of the knife just below the eye of the trout to remove the best part—the cheek **(9).** Turn the head and remove the second cheek. Set them at one end of the filets.

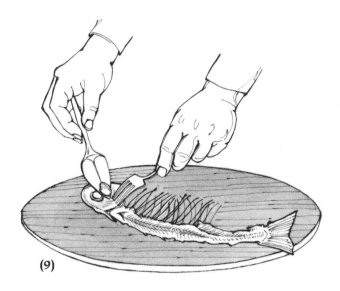

(9)

Serving: You have in a sense been serving throughout the boning. Add a sprig or two of parsley to the fileted trout and present it to your guests.

Cold Red Snapper (or other cold fish)

This fish, with its beautiful rosy skin, is such a marvelous-looking creature that it really needs no further decoration. Garnish it with a few carved radishes (p. 133) if you like, and perhaps add some lettuce leaves for contrast. But whatever you do, keep it simple.

A whole fish weighing 8 pounds will serve 8 to 10 people as a main course; 12 to 15 as an appetizer. Always present it with the head and tail; they are an important part of the total effect. And since many fish markets remove the fins in cleaning, remind yours not to. The fish will be gelling in its own juices, and the fins are a particularly good source of gelatin.

What You Will Need: A large china, silver or stainless steel platter on which to present and bone the fish; a fish fork; a firm carving knife 8–10″ long; a palette fish knife; and two smaller serving platters.

Boning (Method I): Present the fish on the platter with the backbone facing the guests **(1)**. Transfer whatever garnish you may have to one end of the platter.

(1)

Rest the inner surface of the fish fork on the fish, being careful not to pierce the flesh. Now, at the backbone of the fish, slide the tip of the palette knife under the skin and begin carefully peeling it back toward you **(2).** Hide the skin in the stomach cavity. When you reach the area around the fin, remove it with the skin.

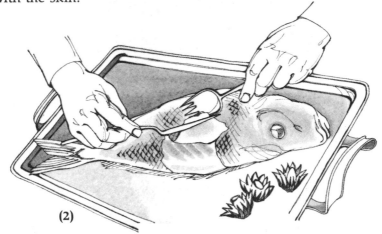

(2)

With the palette knife, make an incision just below the head and another just above the tail. Now slide the palette knife along the backbone to detach the fish from the bone **(3).** Begin at a point above the fin and end at the tail. Push away the small bones along the back as you go.

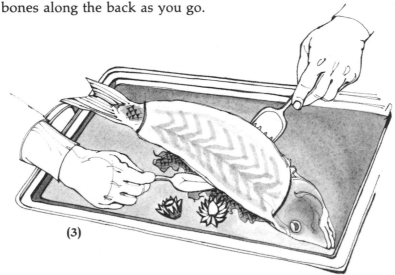

(3)

Beginning at the tail, use the carving knife to cut slices 1″ wide. Be sure to carry the knife down to, not through, the bone, or later you'll be in trouble when it comes to freeing the slices (4). Continue slicing until you reach the place where the fish begins to widen.

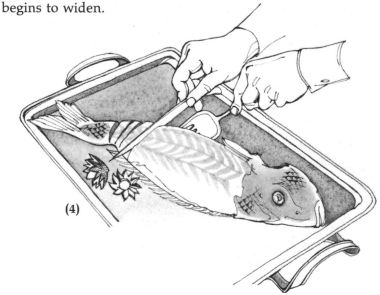

(4)

Rest the inner curve of the fish fork on the surface where you have been cutting. Now go under the flesh with the flat of the carving knife to lift each slice. You should get 4 to 5 of these (5). Serve them as you go on individual serving plates, or arrange them on one of the two platters which you are going to use separately for the pieces taken from the upper and lower sections of the fish.

(5)

Now go back to the point at which you left off, where the fish begins to widen. Make an incision up the center of the fish from the place where you stopped carving to the head, following the natural line of the fish **(6)**. Remove the section closest to you by pulling slightly with the palette knife. We don't serve this lower section, which is where the stomach was, because it has so little flesh. Now slice the filet that's left on the fish in 1" slices.

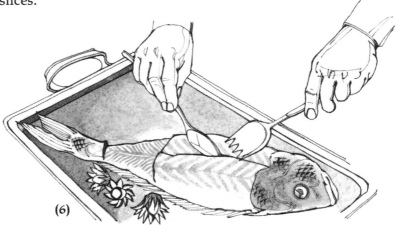

(6)

With the help of the palette knife and fork, carefully turn the fish over **(7)**. At this point you may be tempted to put down your tools in favor of your hands, but persevere. The job is half done.

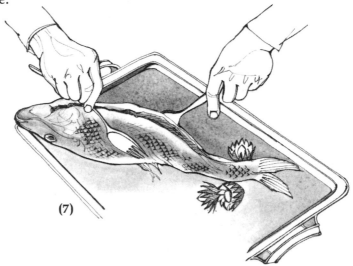

(7)

Repeat what you have done on the other side of the fish, removing the fin and skin, slicing the flesh into 1" sections and placing the upper and lower portions on separate platters **(8)**.

You'll find the skin harder to remove on this side. Just work with smaller pieces.

(8)

Method II: Follow the same procedure as above, but use the palette knife throughout instead of the carving knife to do the slicing. You won't get as clean a cut, but the number of slices will turn out the same. The advantage of this method is that you don't constantly have to switch tools as you go along.

Serving: Serve one slice per person as an appetizer, with a wedge of lemon, and a bit of whatever garnish you are using. Or arrange the upper and lower slices on their plates in the shape of the fish. Give 2 slices per serving as a main course. Green mayonnaise, cold cucumber sauce or a finely chopped celery salad make a nice accompaniment.

Smoked Salmon

This incomparable smoked fish reminds me of the Café de Paris in London, where I worked in the affluent days of the sixties. Tommy Steele played his guitar there, still a nobody, but good enough to get a small round of applause. Still very much a somebody, Talullah Bankhead would come in at the end of the evening. We used to wonder why she was always alone—in contrast to Liberace who, night after night, would appear with his mother and a whole entourage of friends. I also remember Van Johnson at a small table in the back of the room, eating his way through a serious five-course meal.

At the Café de Paris a whole salmon, resting on a trolley, would be taken from its place of honor just inside the entrance to the dining room and wheeled among the guests. I would follow at a discreet distance to watch this subdued exercise in salesmanship and learn how the carving was done.

To be honest, carving a smoked salmon is a very difficult technique to master. I knew one young waiter so paralyzed by the length, breadth and price of this fish that it took him a whole year to learn to carve it. Although it's unlikely to take you that long, don't be discouraged; by the time you've finished a half side of salmon you should be an expert. You will, of course, be buying half a fish, that is a salmon split down its length.

In assembling your tools, remember that smoked salmon is one fish that requires a *very* sharp knife.

What You Will Need: A salmon knife; a table fork; and a long narrow board made of wood or plastic, about 8–9″ wide and 20–22″ long.

Carving: Working from right to left, begin halfway down the salmon to make paper-thin slices, almost horizontally across the top of the fish **(1).** Move your knife a fraction of an inch after each slice to keep the same length and thinness. The secret is to use light sawing motions, moving steadily along the top of the fish. The fork continues to rest on top of the fish; lift it slightly each time the knife passes under it. After this half of the fish is completely sliced, turn the salmon around and, again working from right to left, continue slicing.

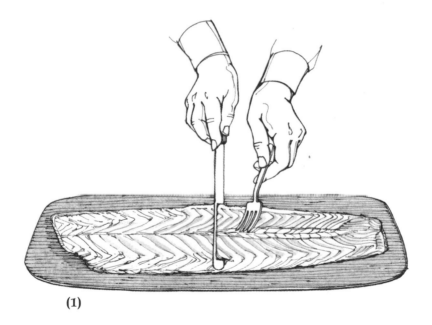

(1)

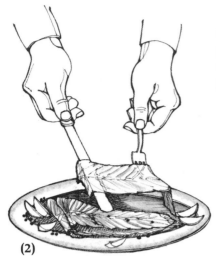

Remove each slice with the fork and knife to the platter or serving plate as you cut it **(2).** Place carefully, otherwise the pieces will stick together.

(2)

Serving: Serve 2 slices to a person with freshly ground pepper, capers and a lemon half. Some people like a bit of finely chopped onion with smoked salmon, but you had better ask first.

Another way of serving smoked salmon is to use the salmon knife and the fork to roll up the slices; then arrange them on a serving platter **(3).** However, for individual servings the slices are always served flat.

(3)

Steamed or Poached Lobster

One thing that Europeans envy Americans is the unsurpassable lobster taken from the icy waters off Maine. No other lobster in the world has a flavor or texture quite like it. As the best New York restaurants fly in Dover sole from England, so the finest Parisian restaurants import Maine lobster.

In choosing yours remember that the male is larger than, but not necessarily superior to, the female; the latter offers the additional delicacy of the roe. You can tell the female by looking for the roe along the length of the body cavity. It is a dove-gray substance, much like the color of the lobster shell before it is cooked. After cooking, the roe turns a bright red. A 2¼- to 2½-pound lobster will serve one person as a main course or 2 as an appetizer.

What You Will Need: A large wooden carving board, big enough to hold the lobster comfortably, with room to spare, for you will need plenty of room to work; a serving platter or good-sized dinner plate for individual servings; a large, firm, pointed chopping knife; a small two-tined fork (such as an oyster fork); a spoon; and an ordinary table fork.

Preparation: Present the lobster on the bare carving board, resting on its stomach with the claws facing the guests **(1).** Its shape and color alone are so dramatic that no garnish could possibly improve it. Before you go to work you might even take a moment or two to let your guests admire it.

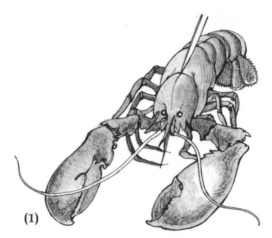

(1)

(2)

Now, with the point of the knife, pierce the midline of the shell at the top of the head, going all the way to the board **(2).** As you go, use your free hand to put extra pressure on the knife. It's not that easy to cut through the shell, especially when the lobster is a big one. Carry the knife through to the tail, separating the body into two halves. Lay them out flat and let everyone enjoy the intricacy and symmetry of their construction.

At this point, it is best to remove the lobster on the board to the kitchen. The work you will be doing is messy, and more easily carried out near the sink.

In the kitchen, use the table fork to remove the tomali, which is the green material lying near the head of the lobster **(3).** Set it aside in a small dish. Now rinse out the tomali cavity. Later, bring the tomali dish to the table with the lobster. Some people don't like it, but enough do so that it's worth asking your guests if they would enjoy a taste.

With your fingers, wrench off the large claws. Bash them in the center with the back of the chopping knife **(4).** Do this on both sides. Now prize out the small hinged part of the claw. Gently remove the meat from both joints with the two-tined fork **(5).** Don't poke at it, just slide the tines between the shell and the meat and pull it away in one beautiful piece.

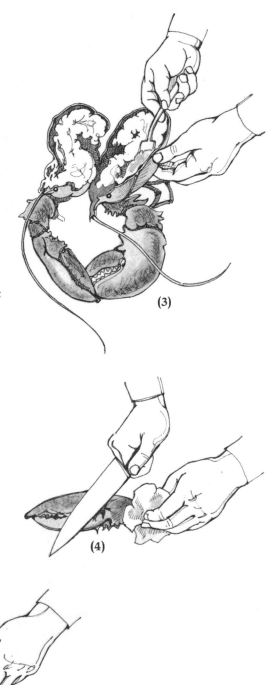

(3)

(4)

(5)

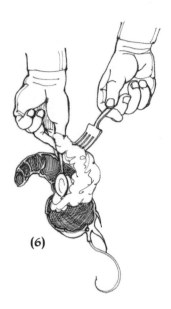

(6)

Insert the fork in the end of the tail meat. Using the spoon to hold down the tail shell, gently lift the fork to pull the meat away from the shell **(6)**. It, too, should come away nicely in one piece.

Rest the fork in the empty body shell of the lobster and use the spoon to pull away the tail shell at the joint **(7)**. Discard it with the claw shells.

With your fingers, twist off the tentacles on either side of the body and set them aside.

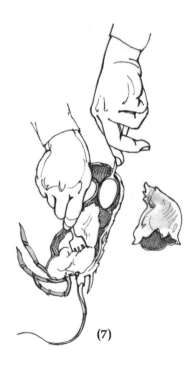

(7)

Place the two halves on a platter or individual serving plate, depending on whether you are serving the lobster as an appetizer or a main course. Arrange the claw meat on top of the body shell where you've removed the tomali. Decorate with the unshelled tentacles **(8).**

Bring the lobster back to the table and serve it with lemon wedges and melted butter.

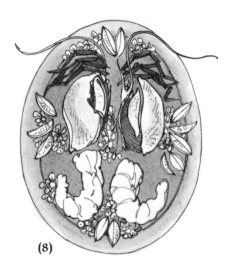

(8)

Carving
Vegetables

Cabbage

What You Will Need: A good-size carving board; a firm slicing knife about 11″ long; and five flexible fingers, or a table fork.

Carving (Method I): Place the cabbage on the board and cut it in half. Set one half aside for later use unless you are going to need that much garnish.

Place the other half cut-side down on the board. Grasp it with your left hand. Now tuck in the tips of your fingers so that only the smooth line of your knuckles shows. Rest the tip of the knife on the board and the upper part of the blade against your knuckles.

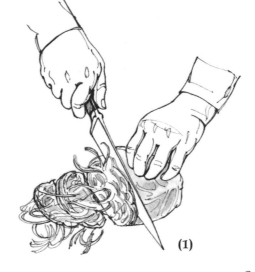

(1)

Now bring the blade down to the board, pressing it outward from the cutting edge to push the slices away **(1)**. Draw back your knuckles a fraction of an inch as you go along to make very thin slices.

(2)

Method II: This method is for those who don't feel that comfortable about such intimacy between knuckle and knife. Simply use a fork as a substitute for your hand. Press it lightly into the surface of the cabbage, the tines curving outward. Tilt the handle slightly forward to act as a guide in the slicing. Gradually pull the handle back as you go along **(2).**

Mushroom

Choose a large white mushroom and remove the stem in the kitchen. Gently wash and dry but leave the cap unpeeled.

What You Will Need: A fork; a stiff knife 8–10″ long; and a wooden chopping board.

Carving: Bring the mushroom cap to the table on the chopping board. Gently insert the fork $\frac{1}{8}$″ into the top of the cap. Raise the handle so that it tilts slightly over the surface of the mushroom. The fork is a leader for the movement of the knife **(1).**

(1)

Begin at the outer edge to make thin slices. Use a chopping motion, straight up and down, making sure to bring the knife all the way down to the board so the slices are cut through **(2)**. Gradually tilt the fork handle backward as you chop **(3)**.

Use for garnish, or arrange the slices on individual serving plates as part of an appetizer.

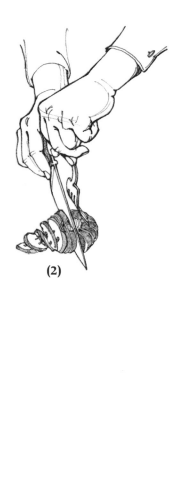

(2)

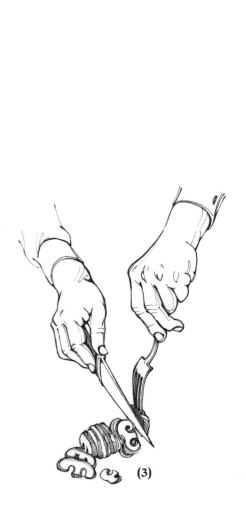

(3)

Onion

What You Will Need: A fair-sized chopping board; a chopping knife; a cleaver; and a table fork.

Carving: In the kitchen, peel a large Bermuda onion and cut off a thin slice at the top to remove the stem end. Take away a similar slice at the bottom to give the onion a surface to stand on.

Present the onion at the table standing up on the board. Resting the inner curve of the fork on the top surface of the onion, use the knife to cut it in half lengthwise **(1)**. Push one half to the side.

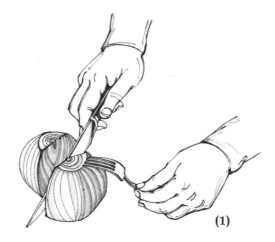

(1)

Rest the onion half face-down on the board. Now make horizontal cuts quite close together but *not* down to the board, until you have come almost but not quite to the end **(2)**.

Next make cuts at a right angle, all the way down to the board in a checkerboard pattern. You will now have diced onions **(3)**.

If you want a finer dice, use the cleaver **(4)**.

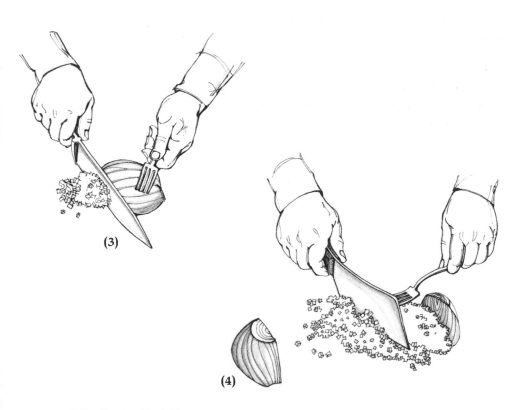

(2)

(3)

(4)

Radish
(or Carrot)

For the best results, use a long radish—about $1\frac{1}{2}''$ in length. If you are using carrots, plan on one medium-sized carrot to make 2 flowers. Do exactly as described below, except that after taking off the top and bottom you will want to cut it again, crosswise, into 2 equal sections.

Something to remember in carving a radish is to hold the paring knife with your thumb well up on the blade, about $1\frac{1}{2}''$ from the tip. This way, your thumb acts as a guide as you cut into the surface of the radish.

What You Will Need: A chopping board and a firm paring knife with a short blade.

Carving: Take off the tip and the base of the radish.

Holding it firmly in your left hand, make an incision at the top with the tip of the knife and cut down until you are $\frac{1}{4}''$ from the bottom **(1).** Keep your knife blade at a slant.

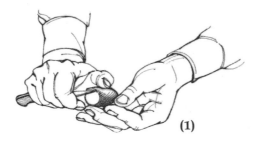

(1)

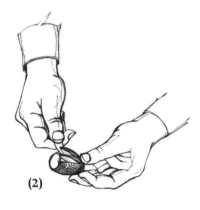

Now move the blade along about ⅛″ and make the next incision **(2).** Repeat these cuts at intervals of ⅛″ around the radish **(3).** You will be able to see the petals beginning to open up even before you're finished.

(2)

(3)

If you want to make your flower look particularly nice, trim the center so that it comes to a point.

Put the radishes in ice water as soon as they are cut **(4).** In a few minutes you will have beautiful hand-sculpted flowers. Kept in water in the refrigerator, they will stay for several days.

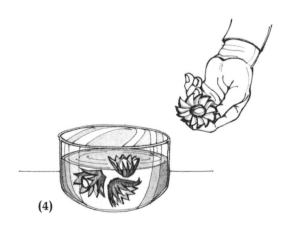

(4)

Beefsteak Tomato

Some people, including a few chefs I know, shrink from the very idea of serving an unpeeled tomato. They think it lacks elegance. As a tomato lover who grows his own, my belief is that a tomato that has been peeled is one that has lost its true character and flavor. However you peel it, either by holding it over a flame until the skin pops, or plunging it quickly into boiling water, it never tastes the same, even after such brief cooking. Nor do the slices hold their shape as well.

In carving a tomato the success of the performance lies in a very sharp knife. So check your knife before you begin, or your tomato will end up a pulpy mess.

What You Will Need: A chopping board; an 8–10″ slicing knife; and a table fork.

Carving: Rest the tomato on the board, stem side up.

Using the inside curve of the fork to steady it, make an incision with the tip of the knife just below the stem and cut shallowly around and under it to remove **(1)**.

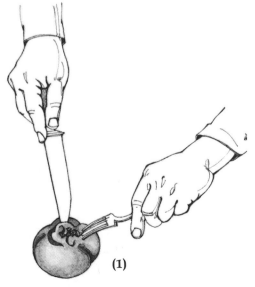

(1)

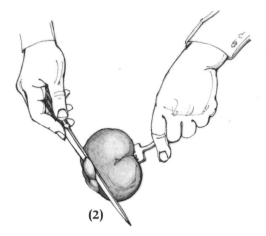

Place the tomato on its side. Pierce it with the fork where the stem has been removed. Now make a very thin slice to take away the surface at the bottom **(2).**

(2)

Working from the bottom, continue cutting very thin slices, the kind you can almost see through **(3).** Use these for garnish. Or, when you are cutting a tomato to be used for an appetizer or as a vegetable, make the slices ½″ thick. You can, if you like, garnish each one with a paper-thin onion ring or with diced onions (see page 132).

(3)

Carving Fruit

To prepare fruit either for garnish or for individual servings at the table is an art in itself. Skillfully done, it has all the appeal of a well-turned magic show. Like the magic show, it also takes practice.

I learned what I know about this kind of carving as a young assistant at the Hotel Albert in Brussels. There, after the last course was cleared away, a huge cut-glass bowl of fresh ripe fruit was wheeled to the table. It was my job to prepare it to order. The sight of those dewy peaches with the bloom still on them, rosy pears, crisp red apples, glowing oranges and cool Charentais melon was usually something not even the best-fed guest could resist. And in turn I got a lot of practice, learning the hard way that round objects roll sometimes in a direct line to the floor, and that even a pear doesn't always stay put. As time went on and my skill improved I found great satisfaction in the lull that would come over the conversation when all eyes turned to me as I got into my act.

Apple
(or Pear)

To peel or not to peel an apple is a question that has gone unresolved ever since the Garden of Eden. Thin circles of apple with the red skin still on are very appealing to the eye, and make an attractive garnish, but the skin can also stick between your teeth. So, in preparing individual servings for dessert, it's best to ask your guest what he prefers.

What You Will Need: A china plate on which to do the carving; a dessert plate on which to serve; a fork; a firm knife with a 4″ blade; and a cylindrical corer. This tool is available in kitchen-supply houses as well as some hardware stores, but be sure not to let them sell you a cone-shaped corer. It never takes away the core all the way to the bottom, and you'll find it's just a waste of time.

Carving: Bring a nice red or golden apple to the table on the plate. Place it on its side. Rest the inside of the fork on the top surface of the fruit to steady it. With the knife, cut off the blossom end **(1)**.

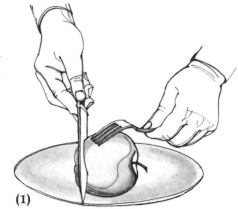

(1)

Insert the fork tines into the slice you have just removed. Now rest the edge of the knife blade on the plate. Press the apple slice against the top of the blade until the fork tines protrude about ¾″ **(2).** This will be your guard for the rest of the cutting.

(2)

Hold the apple firmly with the fork in its guard and remove a slice from the stem end **(3)**.

Reinsert the fork in the stem end of the apple and rest your thumb on the unpeeled surface. Beginning at the top, use the knife to cut around the apple in one beautiful spiraling peel **(4)**. Set the peeling aside with the tip of the knife. Remove the fork.

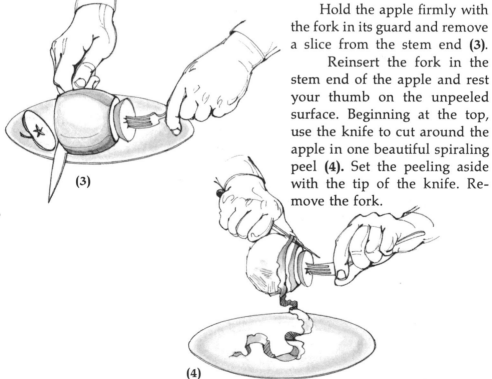

(3)

(4)

Now center the corer and gently press it to the base of the apple to remove the core **(5).**

(5)

Set the apple on its side. Rest the fork on the top. Slice the apple in rounds ⅛″ thick **(6).** If you want smaller pieces cut these rounds in half.

Use for garnish, or arrange in overlapping pieces on a dessert plate for individual servings **(7).**

(6)　　　　　　　　　(7)

Banana

What You Will Need: A china plate and a firm knife with a 4″ blade.

Carving: Lay the unpeeled banana flat on the plate. With the knife, take away ½″ at each end **(1).** Discard these pieces.

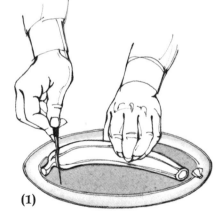

(1)

Now split the banana in half lengthwise without removing the skin **(2).** Place the halves, face down, on the platter.

(2)

Using the flat of the knife to steady the banana, lift up the skin at one end with the fork and peel it back **(3).** There is a precision about this step that never fails to delight an audience. And it is easier to do than you might think.

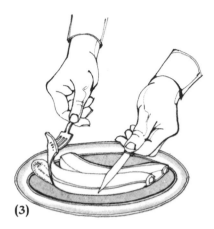

(3)

Repeat with the other half.

Leave the halves in one piece for garnish, or slice each into ½″ sections for fruit salad.

Orange
(or Grapefruit)

Any kind of orange will do, but because of its thick skin a navel orange is easier for the beginner to work with. The first thing you should learn is to forget the rough and ready technique most of us use in preparing an orange for ourselves: tackling it with our bare hands, peeling it with our fingers and then plucking away the membrane. The trick here is to peel the fruit without touching it—or, worse still, without losing touch with it entirely and finding the orange on the floor.

If you are preparing orange sections for garnish or for fruit salad, the work can be done in the kitchen, where you can forget about such niceties as the "hands off" rule. If you are preparing individual servings at the table, do the work on a china serving plate. And remember to stick strictly to your tools.

What You Will Need: A firm knife with a 4" blade; a fork; a china plate on which to work; and a nice-looking dessert plate if you are serving the orange individually.

Carving: Place the orange on its side on the plate. Rest the inner curve of the fork on the surface to steady it. With the knife, take away about a ¼″ slice at each end **(1)**. Set the slices aside.

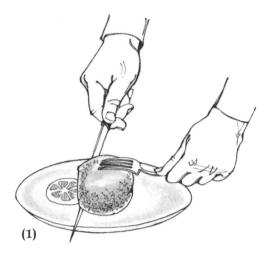

(1)

Set the orange on one end and rest the inner curve of the fork on the top surface. With the paring knife, begin cutting the skin, following the curve of the orange from top to bottom **(2)**. Continue in this way around the orange, removing the peel. Don't worry if a bit of the flesh comes away with the peel. Later, you can squeeze it on the orange sections.

(2)

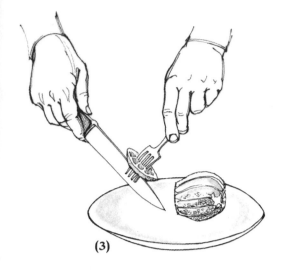

(3)

Rest the edge of the knife blade on the plate. Insert the prongs of the fork into the blossom end which you had set aside. Now gently press this end against the top of the knife blade until the prongs protrude about ¾″ on the other side (3). As with the apple, this end will act as a guard for cutting (4).

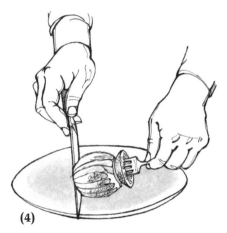

(4)

With the tip of the knife, cut inside the membrane of each segment and remove the sections of flesh (5). If the fork comes out while you are working, don't panic, just quietly reinsert it.

(5)

Arrange the sections in overlapping fashion on individual serving plates to serve as a dessert, or use as a garnish. Just before serving, take the orange peelings and squeeze them over the sections you have cut. Here, at last, you are allowed to use your hands.

Peach

Peeling a peach is optional. Some people dislike the sensation of the fuzzy skin, others regard it as an important part of the total delicious experience of eating a peach. If you are offering individual servings as a summer dessert, it's best to consult your guests about what they prefer. And, if you're not peeling the peach, remember to wash it.

What You Will Need: A three-tined fork; a firm knife with a 4″ blade; a pineapple corer; a china plate on which to work; and a dessert plate to serve on.

Carving (Method I): Insert the fork into the stem end of the fruit. If you are going to peel it, begin at the top, using the knife to pull away the skin.

Leave the fork in place and, with the knife, begin to make very thin slices to the stone. Turn the peach as necessary to complete the rounds **(1).**

Serve overlapping slices on a plate to each guest.

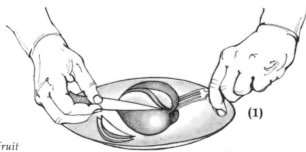

(1)

Method II: A more elegant way of serving peaches is to stuff them with chopped nuts, macaroon crumbs and a dousing of liqueur.

Use the corer to remove the pit **(2).** Insert the stuffing. Then cut in rounds about ¼″ thick. Serve one peach to each guest **(3).**

(2)

(3)

Pineapple

One small pineapple will serve 4 people; a large one, 7 to 8. There are two methods of preparing this fruit, depending on whether or not you want to serve it in or out of its shell. My own view is that not even the most exquisite Limoges or Waterford glass serving bowl can compete with the natural beauty of a whole pineapple brought to the table with its dramatic crest of green spikey leaves and the cut-up flesh inside.

What You Will Need: A large wooden carving board; a firm very sharp slicing knife 8–10″ long; a fork; a cylindrical corer; and a serving platter.

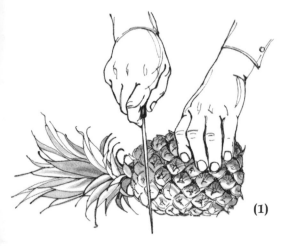

(1)

Carving (Method I): Bring the pineapple to the table standing upright on the carving board. Place it on its side. Here, you may use your hands, for in preparing a pineapple even the most conservative experts agree that it is sometimes necessary to handle it. With the knife, take away a ½″ slice from the bottom. Remove a similar slice from the top **(1)**.

Pause briefly to let your guests breathe in the indescribable aroma of freshly cut pineapple.

Turn the fruit upright. Grasping the top, cut away the skin in long strips to the depth of about ¼″, from the top of the fruit all the way to the board **(2)**. Check as you go along to be sure you are taking away all of the eyes.

(2)

Set the pineapple on its side. Here, you will want to use the fork to steady it as you work; the sides will be slippery. Cut crosswise in ½″ slices **(3)**. Use the corer to remove the hard center in each slice **(4)**. Trim the edges, if necessary.

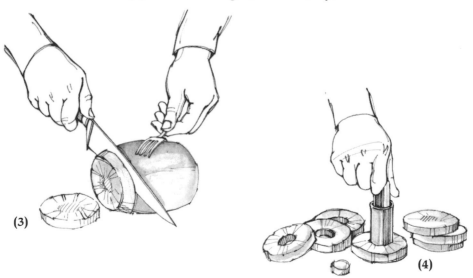

(3)

(4)

Arrange 2 slices per person on individual serving plates and serve, or arrange on a platter, sprinkled with kirsch or garnished with a sprig of mint **(5).**

Method II: Set the pineapple on its side on the carving board. With the knife, remove a ¾″ slice at the top. Set this aside on its cut side for later use.

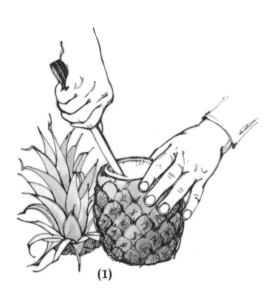

(1)

Rest the pineapple on its base with the cut side up. With the tip of the knife, make an incision ½″ in from the skin, cutting at an angle **(1).** Continue cutting in this way around the pineapple.

Set the fork tines firmly into the core and use the knife to cut away the cone of flesh around it. Set this cone aside **(2).**

(2)

Repeat this procedure twice to remove a second and third cone **(3)**. As you reach the bottom watch out that you don't pierce the skin. Otherwise, you'll lose all those good juices, not to mention the liqueur you're going to add at the end.

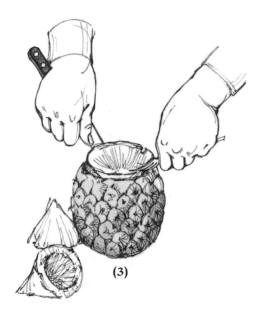

(3)

Use the knife to break up the remaining flesh at the bottom of the pineapple. Again, be careful not to go through the skin.

Place each cone in turn on its base. Slice it very thin from top to bottom, almost in shavings, going in to the point where the core begins **(4)**. Turn the cone as you go and repeat the slicing until there is nothing left but the core of each piece. Discard the cores.

(4)

Return the slices to the pineapple shell. Add two or three tablespoons of kirsch and replace the top **(5).** Set the pineapple on a serving platter and serve from the shell.

(5)